Reviews

"This book exemplifies exactly why Cyndy was like a big sister to me. Her wit, charisma and common sense always characterized her ability to see through the peripheral and collateral nonsense that goes on in a big league locker room and environment. Her stories are filled with tears of joy and tears of sadness and allow us all to relive a transition time in Red Wings history. Red Wings fans and hockey fans will love this read."

— Keith Primeau, former Detroit Red Wings player

"Cyndy Lambert, as we all knew her, was a trailblazer in the newspaper business. Our Detroit Red Wings may have had the largest collection of varied characters of any NHL hockey team ever and this youthful "pup" reporter ... A WOMAN ... recounts her unique perspective of those times."

— Colin Campbell, NHL Senior Executive Vice President of Hockey Operations; former N.Y. Rangers Head Coach, Detroit Red Wings Assistant Coach and NHL player

"When reporter Cyndy Lambert entered an NHL dressing room for the first time in 1984-85, noted tough guy Tiger Williams made it clear that he didn't believe a woman belonged there. Lambert proved Williams wrong for many years as a respected NHL beat writer. Now she has penned an entertaining, insightful and thought-provoking book about what she learned as one of a handful of female hockey writers of that era."

— Kevin Allen, NHL Reporter, USA Today

"Cyndy Lambert's book brings back a lot of memories of the pioneering years when only a handful of women were NHL beat

writers. Cyndy takes you into that world with a collection of personal stories that reveal it wasn't easy, but very rewarding. From her love of a good hockey fight to standing up to Scotty Bowman to the touching story of a Red Wings player surprising her dying mom, Cyndy weaves these stories into a book you won't want to put down."
— Cammy Clark, former NHL Beat Writer

"Witty, insightful and refreshingly candid. Cyndy not only recreates the path to and through her stellar journalism career, but she does so with the same forthrightness and conviction she exhibited every day on the job. I often took cues from her covering the Wings, as she was a true professional (with a great sense of humor) who always got it right and continually advocated for fairness for all reporters with integrity and grace."
— Jennifer Hammond, Sports Reporter, Fox 2-TV, Detroit

POWER PLAY

MY LIFE INSIDE THE
RED WINGS LOCKER ROOM

CYNTHIA LAMBERT

BALBOA.
PRESS

A DIVISION OF HAY HOUSE

Enjoy!!
Cynthia Lambert

Balboa Press books may be ordered through booksellers or by contacting:

Balboa Press
A Division of Hay House
1663 Liberty Drive
Bloomington, IN 47403
www.balboapress.com
1 (877) 407-4847

Print information available on the last page.

ISBN: 978-1-5043-8852-8 (sc)
ISBN: 978-1-5043-8854-2 (hc)
ISBN: 978-1-5043-8853-5 (e)

Library of Congress Control Number: 2017914826

Balboa Press rev. date: 11/07/2017

ACKNOWLEDGEMENTS

This book began as a pet project, one where I could write about cool stories of my life as a sports reporter then print off and distribute the finished product to friends and family members. But as I wrote, and wrote, and wrote it evolved into what you are holding (or viewing) right now: a real book.

I couldn't have done this without the encouragement and input from a team of wonderful people. I am humbled that they took the time to offer suggestions and support for this endeavor. From Tim Reinman and Bob Montgomery who first planted the "idea" seed to Barbara Fatima Clark who had a clear vision for this book many years ago. I need to thank my team of unofficial editors: Dianne Pegg, John Niyo, Ron Bernas, Kate DeSmet, Corrine Auty, Bret Lambert, Gretchen Schock and Mary Kachnowski.

I am indebted to Elizabeth Wagenschutz, my editor extraordinaire, who found time – somehow, someway – to read my words and offer refinement to them. Likewise, Cammy Clark, my intrepid alternate universe sister who loves sports, Maui, coffee and laughing just as much as I do. Thank you for seeing the truth in the words and asking for more. I am so incredibly grateful to Colin Campbell, Kevin Allen, Keith Primeau, Jennifer Hammond and Bob "Wojo" Wojnowski for taking an interest in my story and offering words and support to make it that much better. The final touch came from a "chance" meeting with another former colleague of sorts, Sal Giacona, who jumped in to help me see the opportunities for getting this book in the hands of readers like you.

The universe worked its perfect magic for the cover photo on this book by prompting longtime friend Paul Fayad to offer the use of East Side Hockey's brand new locker room as the perfect backdrop. What would a cover photo be without the person behind the camera? Dale Pegg, an incredible photographer who seemed more excited about taking the cover photo than I was of being in it, thank you for your expertise and for offering guidance along the way! Many of the photographs you see in the center of this book are the result of the kindness and searching by *The Detroit News* photo editor Pam Shermeyer and staff photographer Dale Young. A huge thank you to them for caring enough about this book to locate some of my favorite photos; and thank you to my former employer, *The Detroit News*, for allowing them to be reprinted here.

I am grateful to friend and Grosse Pointe Theatre colleague Kevin Fitzhenry for refining some of my older photos so that they could be included.

Thank you also to my brothers – Jerry, John and Steve – for searching our family archives to find a good mix of family photos. Furthermore, if it weren't for you teaching me with great kindness, and sometimes unforgettable pranks, how to navigate the world of boys (and then men), I'd have been lost and, possibly, may have given up on my dream. You all mean so much to me and I love you dearly.

I wish with all my heart that my mom and dad could be here to hold this book in their hands. Still, I felt their presence around me as I wrote these stories, sometimes tickling me with long-forgotten memories that begged for inclusion. You raised me to be independent, fostered (and tolerated) my strength and fed me a steady diet of humor and love. I am who I am because of you.

Finally, to my son, Quinn. Your ever-present kindness, awesome sense of humor and unyielding belief in your dreams are all inspirations to me. You are the brightest light I have ever known.

DEDICATION

To Quinn ... my light.

CONTENTS

Foreword..xi

Introduction...xiii

1 In the Beginning 1
   Separation Anxiety 9

2 Entry Point..13
   Think Before you Speak 17

3 Don't Scream!..21
   Frozen Senses..27

4 "No One Wants You Here" 33
   Support Within 39

5 I Made It 41
   Did I Actually Write That? 53

6 Cutting My Teeth 57
   Where Am I? 61

7 Finding My Voice 65
   Brutally Tough 71

8 Eric, What's That On Your Tie? 73
   Fight Club 79

9 Understanding Jacques 93
   Comic Relief...97

10 Kirk Gibson Isn't So Tough..99
   Life on the Road – the Good, the Bad and the Scary... 105

11 The Day That Wouldn't End.. 111
   Hold the Coffey..121

12 "No Bill, Just You" 125

    I'm So Confused... 133

13 Celebrity Encounters 137

    Fedorov Gets the Assist.. 145

14 Taking Advantage of Access 149

    The Best and the Worst 155

15 The Ever-expanding Job 159

    The Most Inappropriate Question 163

16 Unforgettable Kindness...................................... 165

    Gone Too Soon 173

17 The Final Push.. 179

    The Sisterhood of the Traveling Reporters................. 185

18 Winning ... and Loss.. 189

    Feeling Welcomed 195

19 Breakaway 199

Post Script..205

FOREWORD

Her smile and prank-pulling ways could fool you, but Cyndy Lambert was as tough as a reporter could be. And during my years covering the Red Wings alongside her, I understood why.

She faced unique challenges as a female sports writer, but just as daunting, she covered a team of strong characters and big-time stars as it began its climb to legendary status. Talk about pressure. Gordie Howe and Ted Lindsay roamed the halls, Steve Yzerman ruled the locker room and Scotty Bowman hovered over all of it. Cyndy handled it all and stood up to slights when necessary, but also understood the dynamics of covering a team. She could be laidback and passionate, funny and stern, and she displays her wit and insight in this enjoyable recounting of her career.

The perfect encapsulation occurred on the celebrated night of March 26, 1997, when Darren McCarty exacted revenge and pummeled Colorado's Claude Lemieux. It was a long-awaited act of retribution, and naturally, we'd covered the buildup extensively. We knew what the Wings knew – they couldn't move forward until they removed the Lemieux shadow with force. On the morning of the game, *The Detroit News* wrote plenty about it. And sure enough, late in the first period the gloves were dropped and Lemieux was felled, and Joe Louis Arena erupted as I've never heard it. When the mayhem settled, there was a commotion in the press box, as Avalanche GM Pierre Lacroix barged past us, loud and agitated.

He purposely bumped into me and delivered a little shove, snarling, "Get out of my way you (expletive) (expletive)!"

Cyndy's professional instincts kicked in and she whirled and demanded to know what happened. She suggested we should file a complaint, because a team official had caused a disturbance in our work space. We didn't do it, but I respected her prevailing sentiment over the years – protective of the profession, determined to get the job done. You'll enjoy reading her tales and witnessing her evolution from intrepid youngster entering a scary realm, into a feisty reporter who loved her work and cherished the competition. In the presence of powerful sports figures, she was pretty darn fearless. In the pages of her recollections – some very poignant, some very funny – you'll see it and feel it.

By the end, I guarantee you'll appreciate her journey and respect her work even more.

Bob Wojnowski
Sports Columnist, **The Detroit News**

INTRODUCTION

While enjoying a casual dinner at the local National Coney Island restaurant with my family and a long tableful of friends, I told a quick story about how funny I found former Detroit Red Wings defenseman Vladimir Konstantinov. I followed that up with a short tale about former Red Wings coach Jacques Demers. My friends laughed … and they wanted more. Until that time I had forgotten how unique and cool my first career (right out of college) actually was, and I was delighted to see their enjoyment from the few accounts I could remember off the top of my head.

After retelling a few more snippets and stories from my career as *The Detroit News* beat writer for the National Hockey League and the Detroit Red Wings, my friend Tim Reinman uttered the request.

"You need to write a book about all of the things you saw," he ordered. Our mutual friend, Bob Montgomery, nodded in agreement.

All the things I saw. Hmm. As I let that thought bounce around in my mind I noticed that I was starting to smile. I had some pretty phenomenal times as a reporter and experienced situations that could bear some telling. It was, after all, a unique time for women in sports reporting – and for the Red Wings hockey team.

While I understood that hearing insightful and never-before-told stories about famous athletes certainly has a market, I wondered if I could recall enough – with sufficient detail – to create an entire book. Truth be told, my mind can be like a sieve, with facts and information pouring in, straight through, and out … forever forgotten.

But I thought I should at least make the effort. I began to jot down my memories on a legal-sized notepad. I began to fill page after page. Before I knew it, my notebook was filled with recollections that made me laugh and cringe, feel sad and elated and, ultimately, hopeful that I could create a memoir of sorts that would be both informative and entertaining.

While my experiences and unique perspective may be engaging for hockey fans to read about, I thought they might also provide a roadmap, albeit sometimes sloppy, for other women (or men) who want to tackle this job as a career … or any job that journeys into uncharted waters. I am saddened that I cannot reach out to four of my favorite Red Wings players – Bob Probert, Shawn Burr, Steve Chiasson and Brad McCrimmon – to help me fill in some blanks or provide happy endings. But at the same time, I am glad that I can bring memories of these men back to life and share what they were like from my perspective.

This book isn't necessarily about me, but about all of the personalities and situations I had the pleasure – or disdain – to encounter. I loved my job as a sportswriter. I loved being the first one to find out about something and then tell the world. From the time I was a little girl growing up with three brothers, I was known as the "informer" in the family. Some would have called me a tattletale, which I guess was the truth on a number of occasions, but I also liked to tell the good news, too; the fun things I witnessed. I loved to see the reactions my reports created. It was powerful! Long distance runners get their highs logging miles one step at a time. I got mine telling people things that would make them say things like, "Really?" or "That can't be true!" or "Yep, I thought so."

This book is meant to give you a glimpse into what it is like to work in a world with some of the most amazing and gritty athletes to ever play the sport of ice hockey (and other sports). It's also intended to make you privy to the trials and rewards of being a beat writer at a major metro daily newspaper. Finally, and potentially the most redeeming part of this whole venture, is to shine the light on my experiences working in a male-dominated world of testosterone-driven warriors, editors and other media members. I say this because, though I have never considered myself a feminist, there are still many prejudices against women – even by other women – performing work that actually does not require male hormones or body parts to do well. You may be surprised to find out what it really was like for me – someone who started in the field of sports reporting, professionally, at the age of 23.

If you are hoping to find salacious stories of married players canoodling with groupies or tales of how I snuck around or hid in corners trying to overhear private conversations for the "scoop," you will be monumentally disappointed. While my career as a sports reporter came at a time when women were breaking new ground in the breadth of what they were "allowed" to cover and in the acceptance of them doing so, I am happy to say that I remained true to my ethics and beliefs. I never went looking to expose a player for misconduct off the ice. I never waged a hate campaign – using my power as a member of the press as payback – on an athlete or coach who I thought had done me wrong. On the occasion when I had to report on a player's off-ice antics or issues, it was generally with disappointment, frustration and sadness ... certainly not with delight, thirst and satisfaction. I believe, because of this, I have very few stories of being treated nastily by players, coaches or anyone else involved in the world of sports, professional or otherwise. My guiding mantra was, "Don't imagine a slight when none was intended." And other than a few isolated incidents, I don't believe I was treated differently just because of my sex.

I truly hope you enjoy reading through my memories and experiences. If there are parts of stories that have minor errors, then I sincerely apologize in advance (please refer to the aforementioned "sieve" comment). Keep in mind that these stories are told from my perspective, with my eyes and ears and, of course, with my reactions and conclusions. Working as a sports reporter for 14 years was a wild and unique ride, one that I hope you enjoy reading about.

1

In the Beginning

I can't ever remember not liking hockey. That's actually kind of a strange thing, too, considering I never played it. That is, unless you count the ice rink my three brothers and I had in our backyard for half of one winter. There, for a few winter weeks, we re-created the glories – albeit, not the grace – of Gordie Howe, Marcel Dionne, Guy Charron and all of our other NHL favorites with rudimentary moves on the bumpy ice on Rossiter in our east side Detroit neighborhood.

I must have been about seven or eight years old when the incident that led to the deconstruction of our rink happened. My brothers and I were hosting about a dozen kids from the neighborhood on the small backyard rink, playing a heated game of hockey. I, being the ever-cautious one, opted not to wear my skates and instead donned my boots with the smooth rubber bottoms. My warped reasoning was that they would offer me more mobility and stability. I believe I was on the ice for only a few minutes before I was checked into the boards (actually, the cyclone fencing) by a neighborhood boy. As could be expected with smooth-bottomed rubber boots, I lost my footing. My feet went out from under me and back I went, smacking my head hard onto the ice. And I wasn't wearing a helmet. No one wore helmets then, not even the NHL players. These were the late 1960s, the days of old time hockey.

The next thing I remembered was my parents leading me into our Ford Galaxy 500 parked in front of our house. After pausing to vomit into the snow, I crawled into the backseat, where I laid down for the short drive to St. John Hospital where I stayed for three days in a ward with adult women. The diagnosis was a bad concussion. I'm not exactly sure why I wasn't in a pediatric ward – maybe no room – so instead, I was flanked by women just under the geriatric cutoff. The food was horrible – Cream of Wheat for breakfast with a glass of cranberry juice to wash it down. Every morning I would give the mush to the large woman in the bed next to me and sip my juice. Lunch and dinner went about the same, drinking only cranberry juice and nibbling on crackers. I couldn't wait to get back home to my mom's cooking, my own bed and my brothers' teasing. When I finally arrived home three days later, the backyard rink was chipped and bumpy. My parents decided that one kid in the hospital was enough for that winter. Gone was the rink. No more glories of scoring a winning goal or pretending we were Olympic skaters. All of it vanished with one stinking concussion.

But all was not lost on the hockey front. Since I came from strong French Canadian roots – notably, the St. Croix family of Barachois, Quebec – hockey was in my blood. From the time I was a little girl, I was drawn to the thrill and brutality of hockey (please don't judge). Then the biggest score happened. My mother's aunt, Aurelie, gained access to four season tickets to the Red Wings games at Olympia Stadium. She arranged for two people from my family to attend many, if not most, of the games with her and the owner of the tickets. Having three brothers and two parents, it was a cycle of about five home games before my name would come up again. Still, to see a half dozen games from the seats at Olympia every season for a few years was enough to whet my appetite for the speed and thrill of the game I would eventually report on as a paying job and career.

My dad, Jerry, was a Detroit police officer. And considering the dicey neighborhood surrounding Olympia, he was the constant attendee at the games. The rest of us, including my hockey-loving mom, Lois, took turns using the final prized ticket. For those familiar with the old Olympia Stadium, there weren't many parking lots or structures designated for those lucky enough to have tickets to the games. Most of the parking was done on the streets or in empty lots tended to by "official" workers. Even if there was an overabundance of parking lots, my dad was the type of guy who wouldn't use them. He had other ideas of where to park. He would pull the Galaxy 500 up in front of a house on a residential street near the arena where a man would be standing, hands stuck deep into his jacket pockets.

"I was thinking I would park here," my dad would tell the man. Pause.

The man would reply: "OK," or something to that effect.

"How about if I give you a dollar or two to watch my car?" my dad would suggest, removing his wallet from his back pocket, allowing it to flop open before pulling out a few bills. The glint off his police badge affixed inside his wallet would emphasize to the man the importance of not tampering with my dad's Galaxy 500 ... and protecting it.

"That is alright," would come the answer.

Our car was always there when we got back to it after the game, in the same shape as how we left it. Keep in mind, these were the late 1960s and early 1970s – the pre- and post-riot days in Detroit – so safety was a concern and a priority.

I'm not sure what I was most concerned with on those walks to the arena: thieves and thugs, or some of the night life that walked the streets of Detroit after dark. And by that I mean rats the size of dogs waddling down the streets and the alleys that ran behind the houses. I remember glancing down an alley on the way to the arena one winter night and seeing the huge back end of a rat scurrying down the middle of the dirt and gravel path. I grabbed my dad's hand tighter and stared straight ahead.

The second obstacle to seeing the games was my Aunt Aurelie. Sitting next to her was potentially dangerous. She was wound pretty tight to begin with, perpetually brimming with energy. Combining that with her passion for hockey left her unable to contain herself during tense times. She had two primary weapons – her two elbows, just like Gordie Howe. Every near-goal, close save by the goalie, or high stick or slash to a Wings player would result in a patented piercing Aunt Aurelie elbow. And being a trim and fit woman, her elbows were like razors. Making matters worse, she wouldn't just give a quick jab, but multiple thrusts until the goal was scored, the puck was safely cleared out of the zone or the penalty called. Accompanying this assault would be a very quickly muttered, "Jesus, Mary and Joseph!"

Other than making it into the rink and surviving the Aunt Aurelie elbow attacks, the rest of the game was pure heaven. It always started the same way for me. After arriving at our seats, my dad would give me the nod. This meant to put on my sweetest face and make my way down to the penalty box area. Once there, I would ask the usher working the aisle if I could *please* have the first broken hockey stick. In those days, when a stick would break, the game official would hand it to the usher, who would then "dispose" of it. I'm guessing not a single stick ever made it into the trash, because there were always kids like me begging for them. Three sticks I remember getting were those of Guy Charron, Nick Libett and Larry Johnston. I never did get an Alex Delvecchio or a Gordie Howe stick, but at that point in my life I didn't care. To this day I still have the Charron stick.

While the sticks were nice to get, the event that stands out most in my mind was the night I met my favorite player – Marcel Dionne. Marcel was a highly skilled player destined for the NHL Hall of Fame. He had an affable smile even when carrying the puck down the ice. For me, this was a nice complement to his French Canadian roots, which also further endeared him to me. It was my dream to meet Marcel. For years I nursed visions of long conversations with him about the game, discussing his successes and obtaining his signature in my flower covered autograph book.

My dad, as has been established, was never reluctant to flash his badge if the occasion called for a little push in a favorable direction. This worked for good parking spaces or to convince a security guard to let him and his daughter a bit closer to the locker room – also referred to as the dressing room – door so that she could get an autograph or two. Unfortunately, the night I gathered enough courage to bring my autograph book and determination to the game, the Wings lost big. I have no recollection to whom they lost but I remember there being a lot of unhappy people milling about after the game. But since it was prearranged, my dad grabbed my hand and we trudged down to the corridor outside the locker room, where we waited with others who had more important business there – reporters, wives of players and probably others like me who just wanted a glimpse of their favorite player in plain clothes for a shake of the hand or a quick scribble of their name.

A long time passed and as players streamed out, I became more discouraged. No Marcel. One of the security guards looked over at us – a Detroit cop and his 11-year-old daughter clutching her girly autograph book in one hand, a ballpoint pen in the other. The guard's act of benevolence would give me, perhaps, the spark that ignited my desire to talk with more players, to learn more about their feelings and assessment of the game.

The security guard silently gave my dad a nod and jerk of his head, indicating for us to follow him. He led us down the hallway to a back door, which was apparently the escape hatch from the dressing room, mostly hidden from plain sight. My dad and I repositioned ourselves outside that door, my hope escalating. Within a few minutes the doorknob began to turn and out stepped Marcel. I ran up to him, making all too much noise, and asked beseechingly if he would sign my autograph book, all the while giggling nervously because I was finally meeting my dream man. At first, Marcel kept walking toward the exit. Then, after giving it more thought, he slowly turned around, gave a sigh and walked back to me. I will never forget how he smiled at me. I was near tears of joy as he looked down at me and made conversation, asking my name, how old I was and apologizing for the lousy game I had just seen. After conversation lagged he pointed, indicating the autograph book.

"Would you like me to sign that?" he said in his beautifully accent-coated words.

"Please!" I replied, fumbling with the small autograph book I had gotten as a souvenir during our recent family trip to Disneyland. I located the first available blank page and handed it to him. There, he signed his autograph (in amazingly beautiful penmanship) right after the "autographs" from Winnie the Pooh and Alice in Wonderland.

Handing the book back to me, Marcel tousled my hair.

"It was nice to meet you, Cyndy," he said.

"Thank you! Thank you so much, Mr. Dionne," I managed. My reply must have been a bit too loud, catching the attention of the media members still camped out by the main door.

"Uh oh," Marcel exhaled.

We were pushed out of the way by the media throngs, as they set upon Marcel for answers to their overdue and pointed questions. But it was OK. I had my autograph and I had finally met my favorite hockey player.

Fast forward a dozen years. Marcel was no longer with the Red Wings but was playing for the Los Angeles Kings; I was no longer a little girl, but cub reporter at *The Detroit News*. There were rumors of Marcel's pending trade to the New York Rangers. I was sent by the paper to the Red Wings-Kings game to write a sidebar and contribute to the notebook to be published the next day. I was instructed to get a quote from Marcel about the potential trade.

Although more than a decade had passed, I was still awestruck by Marcel's talent and persona. Just thinking about talking to him made me feel like I was that 11-year-old girl again. How could I do this? How could I keep my nervousness and excitement hidden? I had to figure it out. It was now my job. So, after the game I waited in the visitors' dressing room – along with a handful of other reporters – hoping to get a quote from him. Time passed and the mass of reporters found other players to interview, leaving me alone. And when Marcel emerged from the shower area (partially dressed, thank God), I was the only one there by his stall in the locker room. It was fate.

I began to speak and he held up his hand.

"No interviews," he said, politely ... of course.

"Actually, I don't want to interview you," I replied. "I just want to thank you."

A quizzical look crossed Marcel's face, and I gave him a brief recap of what transpired years before. It took only a moment and he broke into the huge Marcel smile I recognized. Pulling over a stool next to him, he patted it and invited me to sit down. He asked all about me, who I was working for, how I liked it. Then he thanked me for telling him about meeting him all of those years ago. At one point I looked up and saw that a large group of reporters had gathered around us, all looking panicked and, quite frankly, angry. They likely thought that this rookie scribe was getting the scoop. One reporter, a surly looking man, shot me a nasty look and pointed to his watch, indicating that he was on the clock and nearing his deadline. I didn't care. I turned back and kept talking to Marcel for a moment or two. This was my time, my chance to come full circle with a part of my life. Marcel thanked me for the chat ... adding more loudly that he wouldn't comment on trade rumors. He then got up and told the pack of thirsty reporters the same thing.

I walked out of that dressing room with distinct and unexpected feelings. It was partly the thrill of chatting with Marcel again and actually connecting with him. But it was also a sense of accomplishment. I felt both the weight and the satisfaction of the effort it had taken me to get to that point. Over the next dozen years those feelings would come back to me in varying intensity, reminding me of where I had begun, the hurdles I had to overcome and the pure joy of knowing that I had realized my dream of becoming a hockey writer.

Separation Anxiety

Cynthia Lambert

Working in a field comprised of something like 98.97% men can be daunting and lonely. From my perspective it wasn't that I needed to work with other women to feel comfortable or relaxed, but sometimes all of the testosterone surrounding me was like a constant barrage of pebbles thrown underneath my feet that required constant navigation. In a way it was much like growing up with three brothers and a sports-minded father ... along with a sports-crazed mother. But unlike my household growing up, for the majority of the time I spent as a reporter I was the only woman around.

From the start of my career I had an aversion to being treated special or different because I was a woman. I did what I could to curtail any kind of extra consideration or accommodations because of my sex. I controlled what I could control. I'm sure there were times when players or coaches avoided saying things to me in the same way they might to a group of men. Honestly, for that I was grateful. I didn't need to be talked to like "one of the guys" to understand how the power play was or wasn't working, or what a player felt like as he sat atop the trading block.

My feelings about being treated differently on the basis of being a woman came long before my career in journalism. It might actually be true to say I was born with them. I distinctly remember a night sitting at our family dinner table with my parents and brothers. My dad said something about playing running bases (which we called pickle) after dinner. I was so excited at the prospect of having my dad donning his baseball mitt, throwing the ball and trying to tag us runners. My excitement over this was cut short when I was reminded by one of my brothers that I had to clean up the kitchen after dinner. In our house, my brothers shared the outside work with my dad, and I shared the inside work with my mom. The injustice of this arrangement was obvious to me. There were three of them to help my dad mow the lawn … ONCE A WEEK. Yet, I had to clean the kitchen every night, then help clean the house and do laundry on weekends. As I sat there trying to eat my peas and carrots, my rage simmered. I expressed this as only a 9-year-old girl could.

"It's not fair!" I protested. "Why do I have to clean the kitchen every night just because I'm a girl?"

My brothers laughed at me, and even my dad allowed a chuckle. My mom sat silent for a moment, then spoke.

"She's right," my mom said, putting her napkin on the table. "Steve, you and Cyndy clean the kitchen together, then tomorrow Jerry and John will clean it. You can alternate nights from now on."

She had laid down the law. Even my dad was left speechless. This wasn't like my mom to take a stand like that without first discussing the issue with my dad. But she knew I was right, and I think, deep down, it was the type of battle she had wanted to fight for her entire life but never felt empowered enough to do. That show of strength by my mom as she spoke up for fairness, cleared my vision to see my own power. I learned that night that unfair situations can exist only when we're too afraid or too blind to speak up.

Thus began equality in the Lambert household. Granted, my brothers often paid me to clean their portion of the kitchen, but at least I had the option to say no. When I chose to, I could offer my services for a fee and collect a few bucks a week for my trouble. With my mom's help I had fought this battle and emerged on the other side, bringing about change that was long overdue.

That turning of the tide in my childhood home would forever color my view of fairness, equality and how to speak up for both. My career choice offered me opportunities to exercise this, though not as many as one might think. I can count on one hand the amount of times I felt I was discriminated against or slighted in my time as a sports reporter solely based on the fact that I was a woman.

In fact, when sports reporter extraordinaire Christine Brennan, then of the Washington Post, contacted me about joining the Association for Women in Sports Media (also known as AWESOME), I politely declined. The goal of the organization was true and purposeful: to provide support and connections to other women sports reporters. By that time, however, I had worked so hard to establish myself as just another sports reporter – not a "female" sports reporter – that I didn't want to risk alienating myself from the players, coaches, managers, etc. I didn't want to draw attention to myself or ask the people I covered to change the way they worked to accommodate me. Joining an organization focused on women in sports media seemed to me like voluntary segregation or separation. Looking back on my decision, joining AWESOME would have had zero influence on how the players or coaches treated me. That was all on me. Moreover, I probably could have felt less alone as I traipsed around North America had I bonded with other female reporters covering other sports, perhaps having a new friend to meet up with for dinner or a cup of coffee.

I never considered myself a feminist and don't to this day. Instead, I consider myself an "equalist" if you will. We're all equal, no walls, no lines, no separation. This belief must resonate within. No organization or mantra can do it for us. It's a truth that needs to be nourished and molded so that it can grow in healthy ways. At least that is my belief.

The Association for Women in Sports Media is still a thriving organization and has tremendous support within the journalist community. I am very happy for that. And they could not have had a more respected and altruistic founder than Christine Brennan.

2

Entry Point

My exposure at an early age to professional hockey – and with such fond memories attached to it – whetted my appetite for athletics. As I already mentioned, I grew up in a family that included three brothers ... and no sisters. My dad was a former baseball catcher who spent a short time in the Philadelphia Phillies system, and my mom was the ultimate supporter of anything sports related. My two older brothers, Jerry and John, dabbled in sports in their youth, but my younger brother Steve excelled, playing college baseball at Wayne State University.

I began my own sports career at age 7 when my brothers alley-picked a baseball mitt for my use. It was a mitt for a right-handed player and I was left-handed, but it was better than nothing. Because I had to learn to catch with my left hand and throw with my right, my throwing arm was lame and my catching hand wasn't much better. Ironically, though I was left handed in nearly everything, I batted right-handed and had a great swing and power behind it. To get my bat in the lineup and minimize my crappy fielding and throwing, my coach strategically plunked me in right field, a place where no 7-year-old girl would ever hit the ball.

My parents' reluctance in purchasing me a lefthander's mitt was, I suppose, to make sure of my commitment to playing softball after the initial season. If it was a passing fancy they could save the $5.99 cost of a brand new mitt. But I loved the game so I sucked it up and played the whole season with that castoff mitt, doing my best to manage the embarrassment of my insufficient and inconsistent fielding. My enthusiasm earned me a trip to Federal's Department store with my dad where I promptly selected a sky-blue mitt for a lefthander. That purchase launched me into a softball career that would carry me through high school, playing first base when I wasn't pitching, and the offer of a scholarship to a junior college. My enthusiasm for athletics extended to other sports as well, as I also played tennis and volleyball in addition to softball at Lakeview High School in St. Clair Shores, Michigan. I made varsity for each sport every year, except my senior year, when I opted out of volleyball after undergoing surgery to repair a broken nose suffered in a junior high school basketball incident. My athleticism at that point in my life also earned me several captaincies with my various teams in addition to the Scott Liebaert Memorial Scholarship at Lakeview – awarded each year to a top student athlete.

I received a scholarship to play tennis at Macomb Community College for the first two years of my collegiate career. After that, I was offered and accepted a scholarship to play tennis at Wayne State University. It was through this participation in high school and collegiate sports that I learned about and honed my high level of competitiveness. I also observed how male-dominated the world of sports could be. More specifically, in high school it wasn't hard to notice the difference in fan interest in sports played by the boys compared to those played by the girls. For girls' sports there was generally a smattering of fans, usually a couple of parents watching a tennis match, a few more for volleyball and even a few students, and a bit more cheering for our softball team. By contrast, the boys played to full houses for the majority of their sports, especially hockey. Even the boys' tennis team had a pack of swooning girls who would stick around after school to watch. This ticked me off. And there was nothing I could do about it.

So I moved on, garnering all the enjoyment I could by simply playing the sport of the moment and not expecting accolades from anyone outside of my family or few close friends. That was enough. It had to be. But the whole girls-always-being-the-cheerleaders-for-the-boys still stuck in my craw. It was wrong; it felt wrong deep in my core. We all worked hard to learn a sport and play at a heightened level, yet the girls got a fraction of the recognition simply because they were … girls.

While growing up playing sports helped to ease me into the world of sports reporting, I don't believe a sports reporter – woman or man – has to personally experience the thrill of victory and the agony of defeat to cover a sporting event. Just like you don't have to die to write an obituary, you don't have to play football to understand what a good tackle looks like. That said, having a background in sports helps. Regardless of talent level, playing a sport creates scenarios where you can learn about sacrifice, playing through physical pain, the disappointment of defeat and the satisfaction of victory. It was fairly ironic, as my reporting career progressed, how many members of the media (male members) would scoff at me, implying I didn't know what I was doing or didn't have a right to be there. Yet, it seemed obvious by looking at them that they had never lifted a racket, club, bat, stick or mitt in their life. Or if they had, it was long, long ago. But because they were men, they automatically felt they should be admitted into the "club."

My career in the media began in 1984 when, while attending Wayne State, I interviewed for an unpaid internship at WCZY-FM. Granted, pursuing any job that is "unpaid" doesn't sound like a good career move. But it was for the internship on the prestigious Dick Purtan Program – an enormously popular morning radio show featuring one of the most brilliant, comedic minds in radio. Purtan surrounded himself with a cast of equally superb radio personalities and storytellers. For me, this was a fantastic opportunity. I had been a religious listener to the Purtan Program since I was in my early teens. To work with the likes of Gene Taylor, Colleen Burcar, John Stewart and Mark Andrews was the proverbial dream come true.

Monday through Friday I would wake at 3:15 a.m. to get to the station by 4:30, as the show started promptly at 5 a.m. My job was to pull news from the wire, make coffee and have all of this ready for the show's personalities/talent when they came in. Done at 10 a.m., I would then head to Wayne State for a full day of classes. Because I was on a tennis scholarship at Wayne State, classes were followed by tennis practice or a match. Then it was home to study and collapse into bed. A couple of days a week I would go to my second job – this one paid – as a teller for a credit union. This provided me with enough cash to put gas in my car and have a little pocket change. These were exhausting times but part of the dues everyone said budding journalists must pay.

After working on the Purtan Program for about six months, Mark Andrews, the sports and news director, managed to get me a salary for my work. I made $125 a week and was ecstatic for that. I quit my job at the credit union and declined my tennis scholarship the next fall to devote more time to advance my dream of becoming a sports broadcaster. I got on staff at WAYN, the Wayne State campus radio station as a sports reporter and contributed to the school's South End newspaper, also as a sports reporter.

To help accelerate my path to the big leagues, so to speak, I investigated how to gain admittance as a member of the media to local sporting events. WAYN and the South End newspaper didn't make the credibility cut for any of the local professional sports teams. I tried everywhere, offering to work for minimal pay just to hook on with a professional news outlet. Finally, I nailed a position, this time as an unpaid contributor for the *Northeast Detroiter*, a free weekly newspaper distributed in, well, the northeast suburbs of Detroit. This was all the credibility I needed to break into the "professional" media ranks. And in the fall of 1984, with my Red Wings media game pass secured, I mustered all my courage and traveled to Port Huron to "cover" a Wings exhibition game: my first foray into the professional ranks of reporting, and an event that was aptly named. I had no idea what I was getting myself into.

Think Before you Speak

Cynthia Lambert

Working as an NHL beat writer has its perks. One of the best is the accumulation of vacation time that, depending on how deep into the playoffs the team you cover goes, could stretch long into the summer. Time away from the beat would feel strange to me for the first couple of weeks. I wasn't packing or unpacking a suitcase. I wasn't stressed over deadlines and I could actually make plans with friends and family members. The lack of work to do didn't bother me at all. After being one with my laptop for nine or 10 months, it was good to let it collect some dust.

Usually after about three weeks I would settle into a routine that included going for a bike ride, hitting a bucket of balls at Jawor's driving range or even playing a round of golf. I took up golf a year after I was hired on fulltime by The News. *Many of my friends and relatives played and I loved being outside as much as possible after being cooped up in arenas for 10 months.*

After a few years of playing golf I had become relatively good at the game. I was what you would call a bogey golfer, meaning I averaged about one shot over par on each hole. I was good enough not to embarrass myself at charity golf outings but not so good that I would be irritated if I missed the fairway with a tee shot or couldn't get out of the sand trap with one swing.

This information is important to help explain why I said what I said during the most embarrassing interview of my life.

While hockey, basically, shut down for the summer, it gave each of the teams time to gear up for the next season. The NHL corporate office was no different. Among the services it provided to each team in the league was content for hard copy programs to sell at games. To get ahead of the curve on this endeavor, during the summer the league would tap hockey writers to work as contributors to the magazine-style program. I was thrilled when I received a call from one of the NHL's PR guys asking if I would write an article.

The story would be on Mike Cvik, one of the league's on-ice officials. Cvik was not a referee but a linesman. What made him interesting was that he was 6'9". That put him close to 7 feet tall in skates. I said I would do the story, copied down Cvik's home phone number and gave him a call.

The phone rang about five times. I was about to hang up when someone breathlessly answered. It was Cvik. I introduced myself and my reason for calling.

"Did I catch you at a bad time?" I added.

"No, no," he said. "I just got in the door. I'm taking golf lessons."

Right away I switched into a golf mindset.

"Are you just learning how to play?" I asked.

"No, I've played for a while," Cvik said. "Because I'm so tall there are some nuances I need to learn. So I'm working with a pro who's teaching me the art of being a tall golfer."

I went deeper into the golf lingo mindset …

"What are the main differences?" I asked, genuinely curious.

"Well, because of my height and strength I generate a lot of club head speed. So my backswing and follow-through have to be very deliberate."

Then came my idiotic response.

"I bet you have a really stiff shaft, too," I said. As soon as those words left my mouth I knew I was sunk. Thank God the interview was by phone because I must have turned 50 shades of red. There is absolutely no way of coming back from that one.

There was a significant pause on the other end of the line, then he spoke.

"Yes, I do," he stated. I could tell he was smiling.

I moved right into the actual interview at that point, and he was gentleman enough not to bring up my double entendre. With

with the interview completed, I thanked him for his time.

"Next time I'm in Detroit, why don't you stop by so I can meet you," he said.

Not a chance.

3

Don't Scream!

From the first time I scribbled down notes from an interview and constructed them into a semi-coherent article, I believed that journalism should be called a practice ... kind of like the field of medicine, with a little less blood and much less at stake. That's because, until you're in a real interview situation with a real live person answering – or not answering – your questions, you can't call yourself a reporter. A quick example: I was interviewed by a college student about being a female sports reporter. She seemed poised, had her notebook at the ready, pen full of ink and proceeded to ask me a "yes" or "no" question. I answered, "No." Her response to that was to read the next question listed in her notebook. That question was, "If yes, please explain more."

It can be hard to think on your feet. You may have a list of questions you really want to ask, things you absolutely need to know. But an interview is a living, breathing thing. It can grow in all sorts of weird and unpredictable directions. When this happens you either go with it and ask follow-up questions, or stick to the facts you wanted to know going into the interview. Being able to bend and sway during the interview process and pursue a new angle you hadn't originally considered is a skill, one that can only be learned through practice. It's the only way you can make the story complete and balanced. It is also how you take command of this crucial part of your work.

Or you can do what all too many media members do when there are a number of reporters after the same story or interview: leech off others. Sometimes this is unavoidable. A great example came in 1996, when Red Wings defenseman Paul Coffey inadvertently scored on his own net in the Western Conference finals against Colorado. The Wings ended up losing the game ... by one goal. After that kind of incident there was no way any reporter was going to get an exclusive interview with Coffey after the game. Your only hope is to get close enough in the media mass to hear his response because he certainly wasn't going to repeat himself for those caught in the back of the pack and out of earshot.

It is my opinion that too many reporters leech off others' work when they have a clear avenue to do their own interview. Instead, they scribble down the replies from the source and pass off the Q&A as their own. When these "reporters" write their articles, they don't reveal that someone else asked all of the questions. The saving grace is that the athletes, coaches, managers, etc. know who the leeches are. They know who drives the interview process and who sits back and takes. They don't respect leech reporters. And, ultimately, a reporter's reputation is a key factor in what can make or break their career.

Being able to deal with any possible reporting situation takes skill, courage, time and, as I'll explain, composure. You need to keep your wits about you when, instead of continuing on with the interview, you feel like dropping to all fours and crawling out of the room.

At the point in time this story takes place I was still a year or so away from earning my degree in journalism. Still, I had my *Northeast Detroiter* credentials to open doors for me. Using those credentials, I secured my first press pass in the fall of 1984 to cover a Red Wings exhibition game – a fitting term for what transpired that night.

I wish I could say that I was completely prepared and mentally ready to do a fine reporting job, including conducting my first locker room interviews. But that would be a bold-faced lie and a pathetic attempt to make myself look professional beyond my 22 years. As I sat in the press box watching the exhibition game, my stomach continually rolled, flipped, twisted and turned like I was on the Corkscrew ride at Cedar Point. I was nauseous and nervous. And I was ready to bail on the whole thing, knowing that my shaking hands would betray me during any postgame interview.

There were a number of factors I wasn't sure I could face or overcome.

First, there was the nudity thing. At that age, I was not what you would call worldly. What was going to happen when I saw not only a naked man, but one of the Red Wings au natural? This was a big concern for me.

Then there was the whole, how-do-you-recognize-someone-who-you-have-only-seen-wearing-a-helmet factor? Trust me, after a long game, sweaty players DO NOT look like their head shots or even what they look like after priming a bit for a TV interview. This was a whole new scary ballgame for me.

During the game I managed to quell my nerves by not thinking about the final buzzer. But every time I looked at the clock and saw the game coming to an end my shaking began anew. I also began to question why the hell I was there.

Finally, the inevitable happened. The game ended. I followed the small pack of reporters – none of whom I knew – down to the dressing room at McMorran Arena for the postgame interviews. The other media members – all men – chatted amongst themselves like old pals getting together for a fun night out. I caught a few of them looking me up and down, though none said hello or dared to ask me what media outlet I represented. This only added to my nervousness. But I knew I was past the point of turning back. I took a deep breath and resolved to look like I belonged, and that this was no big deal for me.

The doors opened. I took a deep cleansing breath, put one foot in front of the other and entered the dressing room with my male peers.

This was my first big surprise. It was total chaos. Being a community rink, the room was not as large or comfy as an NHL-caliber setup. There were no names over the stall areas, either, so identification of players was facial recognition only.

To my wonderful surprise, the overwhelming majority of the players covered themselves with towels before and after they showered. When they dropped their towels so they could get dressed, I averted my eyes. I practiced this tactic for my entire career and became quite good at it, casually turning away as if I was looking for someone else – anyone else – to interview, or leafing through my notebook as if there were gems of quotes I needed to review right then. On this day my technique helped my breathing slow to an acceptable pace, preventing a bout of hyperventilation. How embarrassing would it be if I passed out cold on the floor of my first dressing room? My hands were still shaking like I had drunk 10 cups of coffee. And I was afraid to look around too much for fear I'd be perceived as a voyeur. I also believed my reaction to what I saw would betray the composed façade I was attempting to maintain.

I decided I needed to ease into things. I gathered with other reporters to interview Head Coach Nick Polano. As my hands scribbled his responses in my notebook I began to feel more comfortable. My legs were still shaking and my nerves were still a bit frazzled but I was doing it! I shuffled along with the other reporters to interview a couple of players; I even asked a question or two. My nerves were really starting to calm down at this point and I felt as though I was kicking into a new gear. A few more minutes and I knew I could gracefully walk out of the room and give a huge internal scream of success. Then the "incident" happened.

Shawn Burr was an 18-year-old forward who had just been drafted by the Wings a couple of months before. He was just about the most innocent person you could ever meet, with his wispy blond hair, wide blue eyes and broad smile. Because he was so new to the Red Wings he wasn't on my radar as someone I might want to speak to. But as fate would have it, he was my most noteworthy "interview" that night.

Shawn stepped into the main part of the dressing room from the shower area – wearing a towel, thank God. As he made his way to his stall area, his eyes looked over the room. I suppose he was taking it all in after one of his first NHL games – a dream since he was a little boy. Then his eyes fell upon me. I suppose if I were to experience the moment again I would have heard him inhale deeply before he let loose. As it was, time rolled in slow motion over the next few seconds. Shawn, jaw dropped, began shrieking like a five-year-old girl seeing her first centipede. Everything stopped except his mouth. After he ran out of air to support his scream, he inhaled again and began to babble senselessly. I'm hard-pressed to recall exactly what he said because all of the words ran together. But the overall meaning was something like: "What the hell, who the hell … You've got to f&#% be kidding me!"

Anyone who knew this incredibly affable and vociferous man understands that Shawn's gift of gab and hilarious runs of sentences was legendary. It could almost be called a riff, like a hockey version of Robin Williams. But at this point everyone – me, other media members and his future teammates – were just learning about his impulsive and never-ending verbal nature. Meanwhile, I felt like I was going to hurl.

A couple of media members laughed. Shawn's teammates led him away to the safety of his stall. And everyone seemed to be staring at me. I remember offering a nervous giggle, then turning tail and heading to another pack interview of a player, trying desperately to disappear into the throngs while I did my best to recover and assess what had just happened. I knew being in a locker room could be uncomfortable, but I thought all of the discomfort would be on my part. Never did I expect to be screamed at out of fear by an NHL player.

Needless to say, Shawn's reaction did nothing to assuage my

nervousness over this part of the job, but it did prove to be an icebreaker of sorts for me. One of the only reporters to approach me after the outburst was USA Today's Kevin Allen. A gifted writer and reporter who has covered the NHL and all other levels of hockey for decades, Kevin introduced himself to me between his gut-busting giggles.

"That was priceless!" he guffawed, shuffling from one foot to the other, as if on hot coals. "I've never heard a player scream like that at a reporter. This is too much!" He then patted me on the back and peeled away, continuing to giggle his way through the dressing room and his interviews.

More than 30 years later when I called Kevin and asked him if he remembered the famed Burr-Lambert incident, I received an enthusiastic affirmative.

"Are you kidding me?" he said. "An exhibition game, McMorran Arena, Shawn didn't scream but he shrieked at you. I don't think I've ever heard that high pitched of a scream coming from anyone in my life. But you shot right back with, 'C'mon Shawn, I have three brothers.'"

It was then I realized that, at the time of the incident, I must have tripped into some sort of out of body experience. To this day, I do not recall saying that to Shawn.

"How else would I have known you had three brothers?" Allen added, using complete logic. "I'll swear on a stack of Bibles that you said that. It was classic."

What I do remember is that at future NHL All-Star Game gatherings, dinners with groups of media members or anytime the notion struck him during my time spent covering the Red Wings and the NHL, Kevin told anyone who would listen about the two rookies meeting face to face and how absolutely hilarious it was to witness. It was a story Shawn and I would later talk about – him more than me, of course.

Frozen Senses

Cynthia Lambert

One thing that never left me during my 14 years as a sports reporter was my amazement at the endurance, skill and focus of the athletes I had the privilege to cover. And I'm not just talking about professional hockey players. During my career I covered triathlons, marathons, bicycle races, hydroplane races, Grand Prix races, basketball, baseball, football, tennis and golf. I wrote stories about the little mini-mite hockey players who probably didn't know how to tie the laces on their skates but could skate circles around opponents. I saw and reported on girls who could bash the tennis ball around like their rackets were an extension of their powerful arms and hands. I sensed the power of a Tiger Woods swing from the tee box because I could watch from inside the ropes, and I witnessed the strength and precision of women golfers.

I think it was because of my continued fascination with athletes that I was still a bit nervous when talking with some of the best from their respective sports. I would wonder things like: why would Steve Yzerman, Jack Nicklaus or Alan Trammell want to tell their story or strategy to me? It was an internal battle I waged for the better part of my career, yet I was nearly always pleasantly surprised by the honesty and accommodation the most accomplished of athletes showed. Despite this, there were times when there was no overcoming my "fan" nature. Try as I might I couldn't play the cool, calm reporter who was nonplussed by the stardom of Wayne Gretzky, Al Kaline or Tiger Woods.

Ironically, the athlete I had the toughest time speaking to was known as one of the most affable and down to earth to ever play the game of hockey: Gordie Howe. In Detroit, Gordie was considered a hockey god, and not just by me, but by anyone who considered themselves to be even the slightest fan of the game. Gordie was known for his immense talent, but even more notably, for his elbows.

Gordie's career began in 1946 with the Red Wings and ended with him skating for Hartford in 1980. He defined the word "legend" in hockey. Sadly, one of the great breakups in hockey history happened between Gordie and the Red Wings when he left Detroit in the early 1970s after a particularly nasty contract negotiation. And it was the Hartford Whalers – not the Red Wings –who later hired Gordie for a front office job after he finished his playing days.

I remember the first time I saw Gordie in my new capacity as a reporter. It was in the press lounge before a game in Hartford. My mouth went dry as I stood staring at him. He looked at me and waved. I smiled and waved, then headed out of the room. After catching my breath and collecting my senses I phoned my parents to tell them that I – sort of – met Gordie Howe. I was elated. A few minutes later, as the doors began to close on the elevator taking me up to the press box, they suddenly stopped and reopened. There stood Gordie.

"Going up?" he asked, smiling.

"Yes," I mumbled, then scooted over to one side of the cab to allow the legend some room. I could sense him looking at me. I had no idea what to do. No words came to me so I stood there, awkwardly staring ahead.

"Ready for the game?" Gordie asked.

"Yeah," I replied.

"How about that Yzerman," he said, in yet another attempt to converse with me.

"Yeah," I said ... again.

Thankfully (for Gordie) the doors opened and we stepped out. He waved goodbye, and I did the same before making my way to my seat in the press box, needing time, once again, to collect myself and reign in my thrill.

Later in the season, when the Whalers came to Detroit, Gordie made the trip. Once again, I saw him outside the press lounge.

"Hello Cynthia," he said.

"Hi Gordie," I managed, though inside I was elated that he knew my name. End of conversation.

The next season, as I arrived at the press elevator in Hartford and began to step on, I saw that I was, once again, going to share the cab with Gordie. Just the two of us ... again. What are the odds? Despite another year under my belt, I still was hopelessly intimidated by him. I stepped in the elevator and immediately went to the back right corner. I did manage a semi-friendly greeting to him. But this time, Gordie didn't respond. Instead, he stared straight ahead as he slowly shuffled sideways toward me. When we were only about six inches apart, he jabbed me in my side with his elbow.

I burst out laughing, finally able to relax around the legendary player and man. It was the perfect icebreaker. From that moment on, Gordie and I had many fun – and relaxed – conversations. Despite the friendly relationship we had, I never lost my wonder of the man and all he had accomplished and brought to the game of hockey.

I had similar feelings about a handful of other sports legends, lending credence to my personal philosophy that you never truly know how you feel about someone until you meet them face-to-face. Such was the case when I was writing short features, called sidebars, at the U.S. Open golf tournament at Oakland Hills Country Club in the swanky Detroit suburb of Bloomfield Hills. My assignment was to write an article on Jack Nicklaus, who just so happened to be my dad's idol. This meant, by transference, that I also idolized him.

I loved writing about golf; or rather, I loved being on a golf course for work. Maybe it was because of all the hours I spent in cold rinks that made me have a great appreciation for the smell of the grass, the warmth of the sun and the ability to actually see close up the expressions on the athletes' faces. Plus, I truly did love the game of golf.

As could be expected, there was a large group of reporters who also had the obvious idea to write about Nicklaus. But somehow I ended up front and center as Jack conversed with the dozen or so reporters after his round. He relaxed in the seat of a golf cart under the shade of a tree. And thank God the other reporters were there, because I was dumbfounded and tongue-tied. I never realized I felt that strongly about Jack, the legend, the Bear.

Ditto for hockey great Bobby Orr, who revolutionized a defenseman's role on the ice back in the 1960s and '70s. Though he had been retired for nearly 10 years when I first met him, I was star-struck as he walked through the Detroit Red Wings press box one night. He needed a seat, so I nervously offered one of the two vacant ones reserved for The Detroit News *next to me. The Wings were playing the Toronto Maple Leafs. I may have watched about five minutes of the game. The rest of my time was spent talking with Bobby – he was so friendly it didn't take long for the ice to break. He shared stories of his career, observations about the Wings, he asked about me and my career choice. By the end of the game it felt like I was attending the game with a long lost friend. But I wasn't just attending a game, I still had to write about it! When I showed up in then-Wings Coach Jacques Demers' office after the game, I came clean.*

"I have to be honest, Jacques," I said. "I watched the game but didn't really watch it. I sat next to Bobby Orr for the whole game!"

Jacques laughed – for some reason he always seemed amused by me. He gave me a few tidbits regarding his decisions and his thoughts about the game – fortunately a big Red Wings win with little drama. It was enough to get me by. And as I wrote my final game story, the smile wouldn't leave my lips. I had just hung out with Bobby Orr for three hours!

By the time I called it quits on my sports writing career, I was beyond exhausted and was, for the most part, over the novelty of what I did for a living. I quit The Detroit News *in November of 1998. The next March I received a call at home. It was Philadelphia Flyers General Manager and former hockey playing great Bobby Clarke.*

"What can you tell me about the Wings power play?" he asked.

"Well, I can't tell you much. I left the paper back in November," I said.

"Why'd you do that?" he asked, genuinely baffled.

We chatted for a while about the Flyers and what I still knew about the Wings. Then I gave him the name of another reporter at

The News *so he could get the information he needed. Then I gladly accepted his offer of two complimentary tickets for the game the next night. They were a few rows from the ice, in the section reserved for the visiting team. It was my first time back at Joe Louis Arena since leaving the paper. It felt good, but also surreal, to be in the stands instead of in the press box. It also offered me the confirmation that I had made the right move in leaving the paper and my hockey writing days behind me. I enjoyed watching the game and cheering for the good plays. And as I walked out of the arena I felt enormous gratitude that I wasn't schlepping down to the locker room for quotes to enhance the game story and notebook. Instead I could reflect on the game in the relaxation of my car as I drove home.*

4

"No One Wants You Here"

Sometimes it's nice to be the lone wolf. Other times, it's pretty scary. What's great and unexpected is when a scary – and utterly embarrassing – situation turns into a game-changer for the better.

This happened during the 1984-85 Red Wings season. I was still working as an intern on the Dick Purtan Program, taking classes to complete my journalism degree and doing whatever I could to get published. I had the occasional article in the Wayne State campus newspaper and in the *Northeast Detroiter*. I was still nervous before entering the dressing room, but I was slowly getting over that stomach-wrenching aspect of the job. That is, until I came face-to-face with an irate Dave "Tiger" Williams, pretty much the most disagreeable, talentless athlete I met during my entire career.

I had already attended a few Red Wings games with my newfound status as a "real" reporter. I had received sneers from Williams, but nothing more than distant shouts asking, "What are you doing in here?"

After this game, however, I, along with dozens of media members – very few of whom spoke to me, except the Purtan Program's Mark Andrews and a gentleman with the great name of

Frank DeFrank who covered sports for the *Macomb Daily* – entered the dressing room. The Wings had suffered an embarrassing loss so the atmosphere in the dressing room was solemn and, soon to be, scary for me.

I waited with the other reporters in the main part of the dressing room, hoping to land a quick interview with Captain Danny Gare, stars John Ogrodnick and Ron Duguay or second-season sensation Steve Yzerman. I was jolted out of my search for these bonafide stars when Williams strutted up to me. Standing only inches from my face, he pointed his finger toward my chest and started his rant.

"Who do you think you are coming in here?" he shouted. "No one wants you here! I thought I told you not to come in here." He went on to say that the team hated me and that he would personally throw me out of the locker room if I ever came back in again.

I was stunned ... and nearly speechless. I managed to utter something to the effect of: "If you lay one hand on me I'll have my condo in Maui."

Until this time, all of the Red Wings – coaches, scouts and players – had been polite and respectful. Maybe they were ignoring me, assuming I would eventually go away. Or perhaps they were simply being professional. To be called out by this no-talent player was absurd to me. But he was big, loud and scary as he got in my face.

"I'm going to make sure you never come in here again," he threatened, glaring at other members of the media. "You'll never come in here again. What the hell are you doing in here anyway?"

The only thing I said to this was: "My job."

As Williams strutted away, chest puffed up, I looked around at the silenced media around me. No one said anything until one man, I cannot tell you who he was, came up to me and offered this gem: "Yeah, what *are* you doing in here?"

I was stunned and mortified. I wanted to cry right there on the spot. As my legs began to shake uncontrollably and my face reddened, I began, for the first time, to question whether I had it in me to pursue this career. Was it going to be like this most of the time, or even frequently? Wasn't it enough to keep my wits about me to ask relevant questions and write up an engaging account? Must I also have to fight to prove that I belonged and field aggressive threats from players? As these thoughts bounced around my brain, I stood still in the middle of the Red Wings dressing room. With trembling hands, I flashed my Northeast Detroiter media pass in the direction of the questioning reporter. The crowd dispersed, I did a few interviews and left. I needed to get out of there so I could breathe, so I could collect my thoughts, let out my emotions. And, most importantly, to give myself time and space to decide if what Williams and the reporter said to me was true.

As I neared my car in the press parking lot, tears began to well in my eyes. Just a few more yards, Cyndy; hold it together, I pleaded with myself. But when I got to my car, an unexpected clarity hit me. I didn't break down. Instead I felt outraged.

Williams I could forgive. He made his living smashing other people in the face. He was what was referred to in the game as a "goon." Somewhere in his Neanderthal brain I think he believed he was enforcing the code of the dressing room by trying to chase me away. But what really got my shackles up was the response of the other media members. No one stood up for me or stood by me. No one said anything to me afterward to offer support. Then again, I did hightail it out of the room pretty quickly. I didn't realize how quickly until the next morning when I showed up for work at the radio station.

"Will Cyndy Lambert please report to the studio," boomed the voice of the show's producer Gene Taylor. "Report to the studio please, Cyndy Lambert." Gene was never that formal. Usually it was something more along the line of: "Alert … intern! Intern to the studio."

I stopped what I was doing and sprinted to the studio, wondering what could be so urgent. As I entered, Dick looked at me and asked a question.

"How are you, Cyndy?" he asked.

"I'm good ..." I replied, suspicious and a bit nervous.

"Have a seat. Put on the headphones. And use that mic," he said, pointing to the microphone adjacent to him.

I glanced over at Mark Andrews but he gave no clue as to what was about to happen. Instead, he picked up a pair of headphones next to me and moved a mic toward him so he could also talk. We were just about to come out of a commercial break when Dick addressed me.

"We're going to have a chat about what happened last night," he said.

When we came out of the commercial, Dick was, uncharacteristically, all business. To my heartwarming surprise, he and the entire cast of the Purtan Program, were about to stand up for me ... unlike the members of the media the night before. Dick asked about how I obtained a press pass (this was done to allow the listeners knowledge of my legitimate credentials). He followed that up with asking me about my career aspirations. Then Dick roundly and soundly ridiculed and lambasted Tiger Williams to his thousands of listeners. The rest of the show's crew expressed a number of great witty lines to cut even deeper into the situation. Mark backed me up commenting on what a no-talent player Williams was. At least I believe those were his words.

I was stunned that my new employers would stand up for me so swiftly and publicly. It touched me that they cared about what I had gone through. It also touched Red Wings management when they heard this on the radio. Within minutes Red Wings PR director Bill Jamieson was on the phone, asking me about the details. Not only did Bill, one of the all-time great members of the Wings organization, want to control any publicity damage this might bring about – a smart move and one supported by team owners Mike and Marian Ilitch – but he also wanted to make sure I was okay. He emphatically assured me that I was, indeed, welcome.

In a way, Williams' outburst created the exact opposite result of his intent. Instead of creating a mass shunning of me, I was, instead, embraced by the team's ownership and management and even received a few nods of approval from some of the Wings players, most notably John Ogrodnick and Reed Larson. The next time I saw them they asked if I was OK and let me know they didn't echo Williams' sentiments.

I suppose at some point I had to undergo this sort of initiation. I was just glad it came while I worked on the Purtan Program and that it was at the hands of a player who had little to no influence.

Note: Not too long after this incident, Williams was traded to the Los Angeles Kings, taking his three goals and 158 penalty minutes – along with his minus-16 +/- rating – with him.

Support Within

Cynthia Lambert

As I worked and progressed in my hockey writing career, there were many players who quasi-befriended me. I could easily recognize them because they saw beyond the notebook and my job and talked to me as Cyndy, not just another reporter. One of these special players was Colin "Soupy" Campbell. As a defenseman with the Wings, Soupy stood out. While he was talented on the ice, he was the one in the locker room who observed how his teammates conducted themselves and questioned reporters about their motivations for lines of questioning. Upon his retirement from playing in the league, he was hired on as an assistant coach with the Red Wings. One time, during his coaching days and after I had gained my job at The Detroit News, *Soupy approached me in the locker room with a quizzical look. He had just witnessed me interviewing one of the Wings players who chose to sit naked at his stall during the interview.*

"Doesn't that bother you?" Soupy asked, not with judgement but with defensiveness toward me. "Why the f$@# can't he put on clothes or a towel?"

I was caught off guard by Soupy's comment, at first wondering if he thought less of me for allowing this player to chat while sitting in the buff. Should I have demanded he cover himself? Was I being played a fool for putting up with this?

"Well, yeah," I replied. "That would be nice. But I just needed a quick quote."

The "naked" player had never treated me disrespectfully in any other way; in fact, he was someone I could laugh at for his mistakes on the ice and he handled it well. I honestly didn't think he was choosing not to dress to offend me or make me uncomfortable. I put up with this indiscretion because of my inner sense (or guilt) that I was invading the players' territory. That line of thinking led me to the conclusion

39

that I needed to comply with whatever the players were comfortable with. Upon reflection and with gained maturity, I now realize I should have spoken up to the player, asking, respectfully, if he would please cover up. I'm sure he would have ribbed me about the request but would have complied without complaint.

Soupy's attention to that potential breach of respect by the player to me was sign of his role to come as someone who would assess guilt and innocence of players. After years of playing and working in the NHL coaching ranks, Soupy ended up in a prominent position with the NHL, and is currently its Executive Vice President and Director of Hockey Operations. During his tenure with the NHL one of his jobs was to levy discipline to offending players or league personnel. Could have seen that one coming.

5

I Made It

As my studies in Electronic Journalism (now called Broadcast Journalism) continued, I became convinced that I could make my living covering sports. My earlier successes in the field as an amateur reporter provided me with growing confidence and enough momentum to believe I could defy the odds.

During my first semester of the 1984-85 school year, the head of Wayne State's journalism program called me into his office. *The Detroit News* contacted him seeking a student who could work as a part-time editorial assistant in the sports department. I was the first person who crossed his mind and he told me of what he considered this "exciting" news with a smile.

There were two main reasons why I didn't want to go on the interview. First, I was a *Detroit Free Press* reader, and had been for my entire life. Why would I want to work for the conservative *Detroit News*? Second, I didn't want to work at a boring newspaper. I wanted the thrill of being on camera or live radio. Besides that, my academic focus hadn't been on writing, so my confidence level in that arena was lacking.

"Go for the experience of the interview," my disappointed instructor offered. "It'll be good practice for you."

I'm not sure how many other students were interviewed for the job. But I do know I was one of the few sports-crazed journalism students currently in Wayne State's program. I had to admit that it made sense for me to go for the experience of the interview. So I called to set up the appointment at *The News.*

As a side note, preparing to be interviewed for a job you absolutely do not want is the easiest thing in the world. I did zero research on what an editorial assistant's job actually was, didn't look up who the sports editor of *The Detroit News* was and pretty much didn't care what I looked like for the interview. I dressed acceptably, brushed my hair and then drove to *The News* building on Lafayette and Third. My hope was to get it over with in time to catch up with friends for dinner after what I was sure would be a brief interview.

"Just go in, go through the motions and hightail it out of there," I told myself.

I interviewed primarily with then-Sports Editor Rick Sayers. He was a nice man with an incredibly messy office, sections of newspapers strewn everywhere. But he seemed comfortable in his setting, so who was I to have an opinion about it?

Though this was an important interview, it seemed more like a conversation – one I would have with a neighbor. We chatted about Detroit's major sports teams – the Tigers, Lions, Pistons and Red Wings. He asked my thoughts about high school sports, what college teams I liked, how my English grades were. He seemed pleased with my answers, but noncommittal about them. I wasn't sure if he was just going through the motions with me, knowing that I wasn't the top candidate for the job opening but giving me the courtesy of a full interview.

Then we talked about career aspirations. This is where it got a little dicey. I couldn't lie, so I told him that I certainly saw myself as a sports reporter in Detroit. I was confident I had what it took and that I would do it. I left out the part that I *didn't* see myself slaving away at a newspaper.

After the interview ended I was introduced to then-Deputy Sports Editor Phil Laciura and even saw columnist Jerry Green walk through the department (that was cool). After about an hour, the interview process came to a close. All in all, it was a fairly benign experience, until my final handshake with Rick.

"I guess you want to know how much you'll be making," he stated, shaking my suddenly limp hand. Apparently, I had nailed the interview and landed what was likely a dream job for any sportswriter hopeful. But not for me.

"Oh, yeah," I managed to say through gritted teeth. Inside, my mind raced and my gut twisted. I was going to have to quit the Purtan Program. I was now, gulp, a newspaper person. I would have to wear clothes smeared with newspaper print, smoke cigarettes and swig liquor out of a flask. These were my images of what a newspaper person was; all of which were very good reasons why I didn't want to be one of them.

Despite my reluctance at accepting the job, I did. At a deeper level I knew it was that proverbial door opening for me and I had to walk through it. To decline such a job would effectively be thumbing my nose at the gods of opportunity.

My indoctrination to my new reality started quickly, as I learned just what an editorial assistant – or EA – is, or at least what the lowest seniority EA did. My new work hours were 7 p.m. until midnight or later, depending on when all of the west coast games ended. That's because part of my job as an EA was to compile the agate pages. These are the parts of the sports section that are pure statistics – standings, game results, batting averages, goals-against averages, scoring leaders, etc. As I sat at my new work area, computer in front of me, I cruised the results areas for pertinent information. When I saw something I needed, I would copy it from the wire, format it to fit *The News* style, then ship it electronically to be laid out. It was pretty much the most boring job ever – which was still another reason why I didn't want to work for a dusty old newspaper. I wanted the thrill of immediacy, the beauty and lure of broadcast journalism, the flash and sexy nature of TV and radio.

After about two weeks of working as an EA, my initial

reluctance was winning. I was miserable and was ready to quit this great "opportunity." I had just gone from the festive and funny atmosphere of the Purtan Program to the drabness of the second floor of *The News* building. The windows were even painted over in a deliberate attempt to not allow in any sunlight. The only consistent sound was the delicate clicking of fingers on keyboards. Well, that and the relentless cursing of my new colleagues working on the desk as copy editors. I was astounded at the foul language they used. As a Catholic girl who grew up with the constant protection of her policeman father and three very tall brothers, I was in virgin territory. I had never heard language like this before in my life. They scared me!

As my frustration and impatience grew I talked to my mom about my feelings, my discomfort around "those people" and how this job would certainly not lead me to the career I wanted. I then told her that I planned on quitting.

"Cynthia, this is a good job!" she said, using my full first name to emphasize the gravity of the message. "I know it doesn't seem like a good fit for you right now, but give it another two or three weeks. I have a good feeling about this job. If, after a few more weeks, you still feel the same way then you can quit. But in the meantime think about what you can do to make the job better."

It was excellent advice and I took it. I asked Deputy Sports Editor Phil Laciura if I could write articles … any articles. Correction: I begged him. Within a month or so, I had my first reporting assignment – to interview and write a feature article on an 85-year-old dog trainer named George Ward. This was right up my alley. I love dogs and had trained our family canines, Lady and Mindy, to fetch slippers, put their toys away and even to hold still so I could paint their toenails. There couldn't have been a better inaugural article for me to write. After interviewing this gentle man, it took me hours to write the short feature, wanting it to be perfect so that I would be trusted with more assignments. That first article started out like this: George Ward has been dogging it for most of his life.

It was a breakthrough moment for me. Seeing my name in print along with a 15-inch story and photo of George and a leashed dog was an adrenalin rush. And I wanted more. I'll never forget reporter and columnist Lynn Henning complimenting me on the article, calling out that it was my "first," implying there might be more. Lynn is still a prolific writer and one of the nicest guys at the paper.

I told Phil and Rick that I was willing to cover any event, especially those that no other reporter wanted to touch. As a result, I ended up with a rainbow of assignments including bicycle races, triathlons, competitive walking (yes, walking), girls and women's college tennis, local boxing and even bowling. But nothing could prepare me for the request Phil made of me, with the preface that it, "would be a great clip" for my file.

"I want you to go skydiving and write about it – a first-person story," he said. "It's going to get a lot of readers."

Ironically and almost mystically, I had just been chatting with friends who went skydiving the weekend before. That's how the universe works. It presents timely situations to plant a seed in your mind so that you can toss it around for a bit to see how it feels. I did that as my friends described their fun outing of jumping out of a plane. The tossing in my brain lasted for about 20 seconds. I definitely knew that was something I would NEVER do. I mean, c'mon, what kind of mind allows the body wrapped around it to jump out of a perfectly good airplane? It's lunacy.

"Absolutely!" I replied to Phil. I guess my desire to become a legitimate sports writer outweighed my common sense.

Over the next couple of weeks I made arrangements to do a tandem jump at the Tecumseh Airport, located about 60 miles southwest of Detroit. There were two main reasons I opted for the tandem jump where I would be attached to the "jumpmaster," who would be in charge of pulling the chute – the one chute we would share. I would just be along for the ride. My reasons for this choice were steeped in fear. First, I didn't want to jump alone because I could see myself stepping out of the plane, beginning to hyperventilate and passing out in midair. We all know how that would end. Second, the "training" time for doing a tandem jump was about 45 minutes. It was enough time to comprehend what I was about to do, but not too long to give me the opening to back out. With a tandem jump, I would only wear a harness – no parachute. The jumpmaster would also wear a harness, but his would also contain our chute. He would call the shots; and this way, if I did pass out, he would have my back. Upon reflection, it amazed me how little faith I had in myself and how easily I could place my trust in someone I knew for less than an hour – a sobering reflection of my true feelings about myself and my capabilities.

After the 45 minutes of instruction, which detailed how high the plane would climb (about 7,000 feet), how we were going to connect the harnesses and the tactics of crawling out onto a small platform under the wing before we pushed off to start our "dive," I supposedly was ready. The plan was to freefall for about 4,000 feet – or just over 20 seconds – so that I could feel the rush of midair acceleration. I began shaking uncontrollably after being told this fact.

The News photographer, Dale Young, rigged up a camera with a wide-angle lens to the plane's wing, running a remote control wire to the pilot. As the jumpmaster and I climbed out of the plane, readied for our jump and then pushed off, the pilot could press the remote button to capture the last photos of me prior to the dive. It should be noted that Dale was quite perturbed that he couldn't work the photo assignment the way he wanted. His idea was to jump at the same time and take photos all the way down. Instead, he was told that those logistics wouldn't work (I'm sure the camera would have blown out of his hands by the intense wind). So he unhappily remained stationed on the ground below to capture the images of me and the jumpmaster safely floating down to the predetermined landing area.

As the plane neared an altitude of 7,000 feet, the skydiving company's assistant in the shell of the fuselage opened the door. A stiff wind rushed in. I began to giggle. I was not amused. Oh no! It was my response to uncontrollable terror. The jumpmaster saw this and yelled at me to come over so we could begin connecting our harnesses. His brusqueness snapped me out of my odd response to the wind and I reacted as he wanted. Before I knew it we were joined at the hips and shoulders by a series of hooks and straps, and were shuffling our way toward the open door. He yelled at me to lean out the open door and grab onto the strut of the wing. I did this in time with him: right hand first, right foot next, landing onto a small platform fixed to the plane and wing. Next came the left arm and left leg. There we were, standing beneath the wing holding on for dear life with shaky hands and feet precariously resting on a small platform. The wind rushed into my face and I was out of my mind with terror. The jumpmaster instructed me to lift my legs up, bend my knees and push my legs back between his. I did as instructed. He then yelled for me to remove my hands from the strut and grab hold of my harness straps on my chest. I hesitated. He yelled again. I did as he asked.

He had told me before we left the shell of the plane that he would call out, "One, two, three, jump!" But, of course, he didn't. Instead, he yelled into my ear to look at the camera on the wing and smile. I tried. Then he pushed off and we fell like one unified boulder.

Dale, positioned on the ground below with his camera pointing upward, heard my distinct scream from 7,000 feet up. It went something like this: "SHIIIIIIITTTT!!!!"

We freefell for 22 seconds, then the jumpmaster pulled the chute. After a significant jerking feeling as we came to what felt like a dead stop in midair, we drifted peacefully for a couple of minutes before landing gently on the ground. Not surprisingly, my legs wouldn't support me. Every time I tried to take a step, my strength gave way and I buckled to the ground. Under other circumstances, the temporary loss of muscle control would have been embarrassing, but I had just jumped out of a plane! It took a couple of hours, but then I began to feel the adrenaline coursing through my veins. This high seemed to last for weeks. I felt invincible.

My first-person account ran on the front page of the sports section a couple of Sundays later. Almost immediately after, Phil offered me a "columnist" job. The quotes are there because I was certainly not going to join the ranks of our top columnists at the time – Shelby Strother, Joe Falls, Jerry Green and Lynn Henning ... nor should I have. What Phil wanted was for me to be *The Detroit News* pro wrestling columnist ... a job no one else would touch. As an added incentive, I would also receive the TV/Radio sports column, reporting on news in the broadcast sports industry and evaluating how well they did their jobs. This type of reporting was becoming wildly popular, spawned from Rudy Martzke at *USA Today*.

I was completely onboard with the TV/Radio reporting, but pro wrestling? For me that was right up there with the Three Stooges as things I hated most in this world. The thought of having to watch "pro" wrestling as part of my job made my stomach turn. There was no way I could do that. I wanted to be a sports journalist, not a theater critic.

But like my reaction to jumping out of an airplane for a clip, I barely hesitated before I said yes. Forget the fact that I had never willingly watched pro wrestling. On the rare occasion when I had watched it as a child it was because my brothers had a stronghold on the television. But I figured I could work out the actual details of covering the "sport" later. And those details worked out wonderfully.

Without giving too much away, I became good friends with a publicist from the World Wrestling Federation (WWF). He was based at the WWF corporate offices in New York and was ecstatic that I would give the WWF weekly play in a large metro daily newspaper. So he helped me. Every week my contact would feed me tips about upcoming matches and what to expect. Because of this, my "predictions" in the paper prior to the weekend's new WWF telecasts were always spot-on, making me a favorite among the pro wrestling fan base ... which meant absolutely nothing to me.

What did mean a lot to me was the number of published articles I was getting in the paper. My clip file was growing weekly. And, thankfully, most of those articles weren't about pro wrestling but the TV/Radio beat. Every Thursday or Friday I would provide an article listing the hot television and radio coverage coming up that weekend. Then, on Monday, my column assessing the performances and coverage of the most watched events would run. I would also write feature articles about local or national broadcast sports reporters, announcers, producers and commentators.

Also through the TV/Radio sports column I developed a number of contacts in the media and met some remarkable personalities. One of my favorites was Ahmad Rashad. This former NFL wide receiver turned NBC broadcaster was in Detroit in 1985 for the Detroit Lions-New York Jets Thanksgiving Day game. My boss, Phil, recommended that I wine and dine Rashad in an effort to make inroads at NBC. Still only 23 years old, I was completely intimidated by Rashad and had no idea what we would talk about for an hour or so if I took him to dinner. Instead, I asked him if he wanted to go see the Red Wings game. He loved the idea.

"Can you pick me up at the hotel?" he asked.

Wait … what? I was still a full-time college student and only working part time. I drove a dinky Pontiac Sunbird that made way too much noise.

"Sure," I replied and hung up. Immediately, all of the possible outcomes started flooding through my brain. We get in an accident and Ahmad is hopelessly disfigured. He makes a pass at me and I have no idea how to shut him down … because he's Ahmad Rashad. Or, we make it safely to the hockey game and back, but he finds me to be the most boring human being on the face of the earth and my editor's schmoozing tactic seriously backfires. But there was no getting out of it now.

I picked up Ahmad at his hotel in the northwestern suburbs and we headed downtown. I knew that having dinner with him would be uncomfortable. But I didn't think how it would feel to have him sitting next to me in my car for a 30-minute drive. I managed through the discomfort, in part because of how genuinely nice – and unassuming – he was. After entering Joe Louis Arena, my nerves completely calmed. This was my turf. It also set up one of the most unexpectedly funny scenes.

As we walked through the concourse at Joe Louis Arena, heads turned. First of all, the majority of fans at a Red Wings game are Caucasian. Ahmad, at 6'3" and well over 200 pounds – and black – struck a distinct figure. It was comical observing people gawking at him as he cut through the crowd. Many recognized him; others knew he was "someone." We stopped at the concession stand for our dinner. I bought him what he wanted: a 32-ounce beer and an entire pizza. I had a Diet Coke and scammed one piece of the pie.

All of my fears of what I would say – and whether my nerves would make me seem like a complete idiot – were unfounded. Ahmad was friendly and funny. And by the end of the first period, I felt like I was watching the game with one of my brother's friends. We left before the game ended and I drove him back to his hotel. He thanked me profusely for getting him out of the hotel, then paused as he opened the passenger door. He looked at me and began to say something, then stopped.

"No, I want to tell you, but I can't," he explained.

"What?" I asked, my interest piqued. "C'mon, tell me."

He allowed a sheepish grin and got out of the car.

"We'll talk later," he said, now smiling broadly, then walked into the hotel lobby.

The next day I found out what he was going to tell me. During the pregame show on NBC, Ahmad proposed marriage to Phylicia Ayers-Allen. But because the Lions hadn't sold out their game, the television coverage was blacked out locally. I never got to see the live proposal!

Ahmad and I did talk the next week. He explained that he didn't want to tell me in case he chickened out.

Ahmad was one of the many delightful people I met during my days covering TV/Radio sports. Some of my other favorites were former NFL quarterback Terry Bradshaw (a funny and personable man), NBC announcer Marv Albert (I also knew his son, Kenny), CNN's Fred Hickman (formerly with Detroit's NBC affiliate) and ESPN's Steve Levy (whom I couldn't talk to without commenting on his amazing blue eyes).

During one of my work trips to New York, which were meant to help me cultivate my relationships with network contacts and executives, I met with legendary TV executive Dennis Swanson. Dennis headed up ABC Sports, one of the impressive stops in his illustrious career. This meeting, however, had nothing to do with ABC's coverage of any sport, the roster of sportscasters or sensitive contract negotiations. Dennis wanted to interview me for a possible position as an ABC sports publicist. I had already been interviewed by those working for Dennis and made it through those gauntlets. Now it was time to meet with the big dude. And I mean big. Swanson stood well over 6 feet tall, perhaps topping 6'5". Had it not been for his warm smile and personality, it could have been an agonizing interview. Instead, he chatted about the pillow that said "Oprah" sitting on the upholstered sofa in his office. He was the exec who gave Oprah Winfrey her big break, and he talked about her like a favorite child.

As was the case with my interview at *The Detroit News*, I didn't actually want the job at ABC, but thought I owed myself the opportunity to explore what could be a second dream job. I couldn't picture myself moving to New York if I got the position, and I also wasn't sold on the idea of giving up on my dream to be a sports reporter.

Though I made it all the way to the final interview with Swanson, I didn't get the job. And I breathed a sigh of relief.

Did I Actually Write That?

Cynthia Lambert

Accuracy is a cornerstone of reporting. There are a lot of things a reporter needs to get right to keep the story straight: the actual facts, the quotes and even being thorough with the questions asked during the interview. But sometimes, despite the greatest attempts to ensure 100% accuracy, the wheels fall off. During my years writing for The Detroit News *there were times I got the facts wrong, copied down a quote incorrectly and even had some typos that made it into print.*

For the record, the time goalie Glen Hanlon was quoted in one of my game stories as saying, "I couldn't have stopped that shot if I was 6-foot-4," it was a copy editor who changed the quote to make it read like that. What Glen actually said – and what I wrote before it was changed – was: "I couldn't have stopped that shot if I was 6-by-4," meaning the dimensions of the opening of the net.

That printed misquote was a bad one. And I'm sure the next day when Glen explained what he actually said to me, and I blamed the copy editor, my excuse felt like a sorry excuse or lie to him. But that sort of miscue was the sort of thing I felt could compromise my credibility with the players and fans who read my accounts and columns. That said, I did enough twisting of words on my own, resulting in erroneous meanings, that I couldn't be too upset when the copy desk tweaked my words to make them wrong. Two of my greatest offenses still weigh heavily on my mind, but provided me, many fellow reporters, friends, and, I'm sure, readers with a few chuckles.

The first came when Wings forward Sheldon Kennedy returned to the lineup after a somewhat lengthy time on the disabled list. It was probably a complicated groin injury, strained shoulder, pulled hamstring or something like that. His absence was noticeable and felt by the Wings. The team, to be sure, was looking forward to Sheldon getting back on the ice to take a few shifts with his former linemates as he worked his way back into game shape.

When Sheldon returned to the lineup I was surprised that he took a regular shift, meaning he was on the ice whenever his linemates were. This was notable, considering the amount of time he had been on the disabled list. But I didn't exactly write that in my game story. I forgot to hit the '*f*' key. So instead, I wrote: "Sheldon Kennedy took a regular shit." Spellcheck didn't flag it because "shit" is an actual word. And the term "taking a regular shit" is also commonly used. Ugh.

The worst, however, was a stream-of-consciousness mistake that involved someone who turned out to be one of my favorite players – Dino Ciccarelli. Dino was a hard-working and talented player who had a big dose of Napoleon complex, which he used to his – and his team's – great advantage. Dino would stand in front of the opponent's net to act as a screen, blocking the goalie's view of any shots or passes directly in front. In doing this, he put his wellbeing in danger, taking beatings from many a goalie stick or getting nailed with the puck sailing at him at speeds reaching 100 miles per hour. Of course, there were times when Dino embellished the beating he was taking to draw a penalty. In other words, he was scrappy player who moonlighted as an actor.

Because I had to send my first article about the game – called the game story – as soon as the final buzzer sounded to make the early editions, I kept what was called a "running" account, also known as the running game story. This often entailed me simply writing what I saw. And that is what proved to be my big mistake.

On the ice, Dino carried the puck behind the Red Wings net where he waited either for a teammate to get in the clear so he could pass the puck, or for room to skate out with the puck. It is a common play in hockey, but this one was a bit different. Usually it's only a matter of one or two seconds before a move is made. But on this night Dino waited behind the net for a good five seconds before he found a teammate to pass to.

This is what I wrote, just as I saw it: "Dino Ciccarelli carried the puck behind the Detroit net and waited for a few moments before he passed away."

I took a fair amount of kidding in the press box the next game. It was at times like that I was glad I could laugh at myself. Because everyone else was.

6

Cutting My Teeth

Though I enjoyed watching sports on TV and reporting on the coverage – and while I tolerated covering the theater that was called pro wrestling – I was itching to get into what I considered "real" reporting. I wanted to cover live sporting events, delve into the drama, the heartache, the strategy, the glory and the scoops. But in early 1986 I was still part-time and, technically, an editorial assistant.

The News sports editors did all they could to get me the experience I craved. But after doing more writing than compiling agate, the local Newspaper Guild union filed a grievance against me and the paper. Apparently, the union felt I was performing the duties of a reporter, while the paper was still paying me an editorial assistant's wage. It was the union's way of "protecting" me and the integrity of my career path. Mind you, there were no available part-time reporting jobs and I couldn't work full-time because I still hadn't earned my college degree.

From my point of view, the union was preventing me from getting the experience I needed. And I was furious when told I would only be able to do periodic reporting until I got my degree. In the meantime, I was back on the desk, working until 2 a.m. to include those important west coast scores in the late edition.

As I labored through my final year of schooling – grades weren't a priority for me anymore, as I had been told I would be made full time as soon as I graduated regardless of my grade point average – I was still able to land a gem assignment or two. One came during the summer of 1986 when I was sent to write a sidebar at the Detroit Tigers game at historic Tiger Stadium. As much as I loved hockey, baseball was and will always be my first "sport" love. To be on the field as the Tigers took batting practice was surreal and thrilling. It was one of many times in my career I had to talk myself down from freaking out about where I was and what was expected of me. I needed to keep my composure and act like a professional, even though I felt like a little kid.

As I watched batting practice, someone came up from behind me.

"Hello there," came the greeting. The voice was rich and warm, like molasses and ever so familiar. It was legendary Tigers radio play-by-play man Ernie Harwell. A gentler, kinder man will never be found. Ernie introduced himself and proceeded to ask all about me in a genuinely interested manner. We chatted about the legendary author of *Gone with the Wind*, Margaret Mitchell, and how he and his brother were her paperboys down in the old South. We talked baseball, reporting and life. Now I was floating even more. But I had work to do and Scarlett O'Hara and Rhett Butler would not make good sidebar fodder.

I still needed a story for the early editions. My idea was to focus on second baseman Lou Whitaker, who, at that point, was slumping. Because I was new to the reporting world, I didn't know that Whitaker rarely spoke to the media, particularly before a game. Indeed, ignorance can be a blessing. I asked "Sweet Lou" for an interview as he stood waiting to take batting practice. He smiled. That's it. He just smiled. What the heck did that mean?

So I waited. And waited. Batting practice was nearly over and the on-field security team personnel were starting to clear the area of the clutter of reporters. Oh no! What if Lou changes his mind now? I had completely neglected to arrange for a plan B. I would have to trudge up to the press box and tell our beat writer Tom Gage that I had nothing. They would have to pull a story from the Associated Press wire to fill the gap left by my inexperienced decision.

Another glance to Lou gave me no indication of which way he was leaning. Then he made a move in my direction, which also happened to be the direction of the Tigers dugout. As he passed by me, he turned and spoke.

"Do you still want to talk?" he asked.

"Uh … yes," I managed.

"C'mon over here; we can sit and talk," he said, leading me to the dugout. I was in the dugout at Tiger Stadium! As I conducted the interview, many of the other Tigers players gave me sideways glances, but Sweet Lou kept talking and I kept writing.

When I got to the press box and told Tom that I had a Lou Whitaker sidebar he stopped.

"He talked to you?" he asked.

"Yeah," I replied.

"That's great! Write it up," Tom said, and I think he even patted me on the back.

At that moment I felt the rush of "getting the story." It was an intoxicating feeling I would chase for more than a decade.

That winter I officially graduated from Wayne State. The night of commencements I was given the option of actually *covering* the Red Wings game … not sidebar writing, but actually being the reporter of record … or go to my commencement. There was no wrestling with that decision. I opted out of the cap and gown ceremony, grabbed my notebook and pen, along with the TR-80 Radio Shack "computer," which would soon earn the moniker Trash-80, and headed to Joe Louis Arena to do my job.

I was fortunate that both of my parents understood the enormity of covering the Wings game, and they put up no protests about not attending the graduation ceremony. From my perspective, I pursued my degree in journalism so that I could work in the field. Why would I choose to celebrate my victory of attaining my Bachelor's degree by walking down an aisle instead of putting into practice what I had been trained to do?

The sports editors at *The News* kept their word, and I was made a full-time reporter as soon as I graduated. It opened up more possibilities than I ever could have imagined, setting the stage for an amazing career.

Where Am I?

Cynthia Lambert

It's really annoying when people who have a dream career like mine complain and say, "It's not as glamorous as it looks," or, "If only I had a nine-to-five job with a predictable schedule."

Yeah, right. Because chatting every day with some of the best athletes in the world, traveling all over North America, staying in five-star hotels and getting a byline in what was then the largest daily newspaper in Detroit is such a drag.

Knowing this, I was always reluctant to complain to anyone about how tired I was, how I didn't want to travel to Washington, D.C. (because we weren't actually in D.C. proper, but in Landover, Maryland) or Buffalo or Winnipeg or Edmonton, or that I just wanted to go to my nephew's birthday party or meet some friends for dinner ... then go back home for a quiet night watching anything but hockey, or any sport for that matter.

The fact that people didn't want to hear my griping was driven home in the spring of 1991 as the Wings were entering the playoffs. My cousin Derrick was getting married to his sweetheart Danita in Maui near the end of April. I desperately wanted to go to the wedding. The only way this was possible was if the Wings lost to the St. Louis Blues in the first round. That would free me up in time to hop a flight to Maui to watch the nuptials and enjoy my favorite place on Earth. The team had a sub-.500 season so it was not unreasonable that they would – or should – lose.

I had arranged for free airline tickets to Maui for my mom and dad, compliments of some of my million miles logged on Northwest Airlines. I also had enough to get a free ticket for myself if my game plan played out as I hoped. For weeks I dreamed of sitting on the beach, watching the waves roll in, spotting humpback whales coming up for air, cheering on the surfers as they twisted and turned in the swells off Kapalua. Just imagining being there was like heaven to me. After a long season of travel and deadlines, I was exhausted. I was done. I needed a break. When I voiced this to my mother, she bristled.

"What do you mean you want them to lose?" she exclaimed. "That's pretty selfish of you, Cyndy."

Selfish? She wanted to watch more playoff hockey. Who was being selfish?

"Really mom?" I said, exasperated. "I'm tired, and I want to see Derrick get married. I want to go to Hawaii."

She said I should stop complaining and be grateful for the job I had. It was then I realized the full extent of her love of the Red Wings. Until that moment it didn't occur to me how deeply her loyalty to the Red wings ran. It also put into perspective my commitment to doing my job well, understanding that I had signed up for it. No one was forcing me to keep this job, so I might as well accept it and appreciate the journey.

But the Red Wings did lose in the first round that year. Ha! And I was able to go to Maui. And my mom was very glad I was there.

The next season I experienced something that was a forewarning about how much travel I could handle. I had been on every road trip with the team, not taking a single day off for months. I was weary of the road, tired of seeing and lugging my suitcase, and I was frustrated at being in hotel rooms where I couldn't crack a window to allow in some fresh air. On this morning I woke before my wakeup call sounded. The sun was just beginning to rise. I could make out the furniture in the room but had no idea where I was. I began to panic. Where the heck was I? Was I going to be late for the practice or a flight?

I had been in so many cities for the past couple of weeks that I couldn't remember which airport I had landed in last.

Think, Cyndy, think. As I scanned the room I realized that it was familiar and comfortable.

"It must be a Norris Division city," I reasoned, since the Wings played more games in each Norris Division team's city each season. That narrowed it down some. It was either Toronto, Chicago, Minnesota or St. Louis. As I began to wake up more, the pictures on the walls, the windows and curtains, everything started to fall into place like a puzzle. Then it dawned on me.

I was home.

I picked up the phone, called my boss and told him that I needed a couple of days off, starting immediately.

Finding My Voice

As I have already said, journalism should be called a practice. There is no way to teach anyone about all of the types of situations that can pop up as you cover a story.

I was lucky. I covered sports. I didn't have to deal with issues of my personal safety (though some of the waits for a cab at the old Chicago Stadium got a bit tense), unsavory characters (only a negligible amount of offensive players) or the challenges of putting up with the exploits of politicians (dealing with the team owners and general managers was difficult enough for me).

My biggest and most consistent challenge was that nagging feeling that I was different than the rest of the reporters. Which, of course, I was. And my "difference" could not be hidden. I was a woman in a man's world. There was no getting around it.

It's important to keep in mind that in the mid-1980s – when I started on my career path – there were very few female sports reporters, and even fewer in the Motor City. Detroit sports broadcast journalist Anne Doyle certainly paved the way for me and others. She worked at the CBS affiliate, Channel 2, from 1978-83 before vaulting onto the national scene. She was a role model who earned kudos because of her talent, vast knowledge of sports and reputation as a professional. Though she may have gotten a foot in the door

65

because she was the daughter of legendary Detroit sportscaster Vince Doyle, it was up to her to blaze her own career path. Her dad was not there holding her hand as she walked into locker rooms or conducted her hundreds of interviews with athletes, managers, owners, scouts, trainers and coaches.

Female journalist Johnette Howard worked at the *Detroit Free Press* covering the NBA and Olympics right when I began my job at *The News*. Because she was a print reporter, and because of her friendly and easygoing personality, Johnette was more a role model for me. Though we didn't see each other often, she was always kind and encouraging when our paths would cross. It's no surprise that she has continued to build on her career as a premier sports reporter.

But after Johnette and Anne, there were no other prominent female sports reporters in Detroit, or at least no woman who achieved beat writer or columnist status in the newspaper business in Detroit. Despite this, many of us, including fellow *Detroit News* reporter Lisa Dillman, were knocking at that door in the mid-'80s.

Unlike my male counterparts, I had decisions to make regarding how I would present myself as I did my job. I grew up as a jock, so talking sports was not going to be a problem. How I came across to the players, managers, coaches, etc. was my concern. I wanted to be professional, but open; businesslike, but warm. But I didn't want to be too open and warm and give off a vibe that wasn't my intention. Of course I was overthinking it, as I tend to do with all important things in my life.

I remember receiving sporadic advice from well-meaning reporters – most of whom were men, but also a smattering of women – suggesting I dress in a manly or gender-neutral fashion and eschew jewelry. This was perplexing, as if trying to cover up that I was a woman would fool the athletes into thinking I was man and they would treat me like one of the guys. Seriously? Apparently, by creating an androgynous look all would be well and no one would have to deal with the fact that I had female body parts underneath my sweater and jeans.

The most ludicrous suggestion I received was one steeped in deceit. It was recommended that I wear a fake wedding band so that those I worked with wouldn't think I was there to get a date. It must have taken serious time to come up with this winner of an idea. After a goalie gives up six goals on 20 shots, has a pulled groin and knows he may be headed to the minors or the trading block, I highly doubt he's looking to see if a new reporter is "available."

Both of these suggestions struck me as ironic. As a reporter, you are – or should be – a seeker of the truth. You want your interviewees to be honest with you. These crazy suggestions set me up to be a liar and deceive the same people from whom I expected the truth.

I continued wearing what I wanted, which was usually jeans because they were more comfortable when climbing stairs to press boxes located near the rafters or standing next to sweaty athletes who might spit inches away from me. And, since I was not married while I worked at the paper, I wore no wedding ring.

This is not to say my path toward equality in the dressing room was achieved by careful attention to my wardrobe. What is referred to as "equality" in the locker room was achieved when "equal" access was allowed to women. But effectiveness as a reporter is achieved by getting the facts right, conducting respectful interviews, writing balanced accounts and working hard.

There were a few occasions when I had to stand up for myself to those who were less than accepting of me. But even then, I tried to see it from their perspective. If I had grown up with different parents, in a different setting and with different interests, I may also have scoffed at a woman wanting to go inside a locker room. If I were a man, or one of the athletes, I may not have liked a young woman – or any woman – coming into the locker room. But I grew up with three brothers, an athletic father and a mother who was a sports fanatic. My personality drove me to succeed in sports, school and life. When I think about it that way, it was completely natural that I would choose sports reporting as my profession and I am still grateful that I entered the field at a time when a career was possible, yet still new.

Once all of the "equality" for men and women in the locker room issues were decided, I still had to deal with situations that were unique to me. And some of them turned out to be comical.

One of my favorite and most memorable situations involved Detroit Pistons "Bad Boy" Rick Mahorn. I was sent to write a sidebar at a regular season game, my first foray into pro basketball coverage. It was amazing to watch the game from press row – literally a row of tables and chairs on the hardwood, just beyond the court. I had never been this close to the action and it was mesmerizing. But as fascinating as it was to watch these athletes up close, I was still dealing with butterflies in my stomach. As soon as the game ended, I would have to go into the locker room where I knew no one and no one knew me. This made me nervous.

"What is the reaction going to be?"

"Will I find the players I need to speak to?"

"Will I ever find my way back to press row?" (I have a knack for getting lost).

Entering the Pistons locker room, I noticed how much calmer it was – and how much larger the ratio of media-to-players was. It had not occurred to me until that moment how the team size of basketball vs. hockey would impact the atmosphere in the dressing room.

I spoke with Bill Laimbeer and Kelly Tripucka before wandering over to where Rick Mahorn sat. Oddly and luckily, no other media members were around. I introduced myself and he politely motioned for me to sit down on the stool next to him.

"Whoa, this is nice!" I thought to myself, reveling in my immediate acceptance by Mahorn. I started the interview. He answered every question politely but with terms of endearment that just weren't, well, appropriate. He used words such as, "baby," "sugar," and "sweetheart." But I'll be darned if he didn't say them so nicely that it was hard for me to be offended. I knew he wasn't saying them to come on to me or to set me off balance. It was him being his charming self. But I couldn't let it continue.

"Cynthia ... or Cyndy," I replied after he called me sweetheart.

"Oh, baby, you don't have to say that," he replied, offering his huge grin.

"Yes. Yes I do," I said, laughing but holding my ground.

"Aw shoot," he said. "I can't call you sugar either?"

"Nope."

We both laughed and I continued with the interview. And Rick Mahorn became one of my new favorite people in the world of sports.

I feel this story is important because had I taken offense at Mahorn's unfiltered way of speaking, the evening could have erupted into a confrontation. It may have earned me more recognition in the ranks of reporting, but would have simultaneously created negative attention for Mahorn, who meant no harm by his comments. Instead, I treated him like any other guy and established the boundaries of our relationship. I didn't give energy to a belief that he was trying to unnerve me or be disrespectful. If he was, I didn't bite. But I truthfully don't think he meant anything untoward at all. Because of my decisions, the interview ended up being one of the most jovial and interesting of my career.

Throughout my career I encountered only a handful of challenging situations with unaccepting people, most of which were quick to resolve or ignore. Overall, I was free to do my job without prejudice or obstacles.

That said, I found life on the road to be laced with a bit of loneliness. While the male reporters gathered for dinners or nights out, I was not invited – nor would I want to go, I suppose. Periodically, I would have breakfast with Wings radio announcers Bruce Martyn and Paul Woods, but aside from that I was on my own. As the years clicked off I became friends with reporters in the different cities. Some of my favorite fellow reporters were Jim Kelley and Tim Campbell, in Buffalo and Winnipeg, respectively. Jim was also president of the Hockey Writers' Association, so we had some great conversations about the history of reporters, coaches and players. And I could always count on Tim to line up something fun to do in Winnipeg, driving his sedan through the snowy tunnels – also called streets – in the frozen north that was his city.

Others, including pretty much the entire New Jersey and New York reporting contingent, made me look forward to my travels there. This group included fellow female reporter Sherry Ross, who covered the Devils, Frank Brown and John Dellapina (both of whom later gave up their notebooks and took jobs in the NHL's New York front office) and the reporters in Edmonton, Calgary, St. Louis and Toronto. It was always great to travel to Los Angeles, Boston and Tampa Bay to see fellow female writers Helene Elliott, Karen Crouse, Nancy Marapese and Cammy Clark. The camaraderie of these reporters made life on the road easier and helped me to expand my network, something that would come into play later in many big ways.

Brutally Tough

Cynthia Lambert

As a hockey reporter in the days when fighting between players was not only permitted by the National Hockey League but encouraged and celebrated, the league was sprinkled with its fair share of players referred to as enforcers, or goons. These were the guys who would protect the more talented players by slamming into opponents, cross checking or high sticking them ... and then, the penultimate, dropping the gloves and slugging it out. Some of the best enforcers in the league during my tenure included Bob Probert (who had substantial talent as well), Joe Kocur, Marty McSorley, Mike Peluso, Troy Crowder, Jim Kyte, Tie Domi and Craig Berube. Since he spent the majority of his career in Detroit, I got to see just how tough Probert was on the ice. I marveled at his style of fighting, which was to take as many punches as he could tolerate, tiring out his opponent. Then he would reach into his reserve and manhandle the poor sap who chose to take him on.

But as tough as Probert was on the ice, off of it I witnessed a playful, reserved and fun-loving guy. He never struck an imposing figure to me in the locker room, nor did the others I've mentioned – except for Berube. In the late-1980s and very early '90s, Berube played for the Philadelphia Flyers, who always seemed to field a rugged lineup to keep the Broad Street Bullies reputation, firmly established in the 1970s, intact. The Wings were in Philadelphia for a couple of days as part of a longer road trip. Because of that, I had the pleasure to visit the Flyers' practice rink, which was out in the suburbs somewhere. It was the dead of winter and the temperature was in the 20s, if not the teens. As the Red Wings team bus arrived for practice, the Flyers were just wrapping up theirs. I conducted my interviews of the Flyers, finding it hard to shed the chill from outside. As the Wings took to the ice, I realized something very troubling. I could see my breath ... inside the arena. Because of the amount of hockey practices and games I'd attended by that point, I was used to arenas – big ones, small ones, nice ones, smelly ones. But I had never before been in a rink this cold. It actually felt colder inside the rink than outside.

As I watched the Wings skate around, a figure emerged from the Flyers dressing room. He wore jeans and a sleeveless white T-shirt. Casually flung over one shoulder was a black leather jacket; black boots donned his feet. His hair – dark, long and wet – was combed back away from his face in an extreme style, accenting his high, prominent cheekbones. It was Craig Berube. As he walked – more like strutted – past me, I noticed that he wasn't shivering at all and had no visible goosebumps. His breath created a steady fog around his face as he took one long stride after another and out the door.

"Oh my God!" I thought to myself, jaw dropping in amazement.

Because Berube's on-ice specialty was more enforcer than skilled player, I don't ever recall interviewing him. But I had a clear understanding of who he was after experiencing those 10 seconds in the frigid rink – the toughest guy I ever saw.

8

Eric, What's That On Your Tie?

A favorite time of the hockey season for me was always the Amateur Entry Draft, held in June. Though its timing couldn't have been worse, coming immediately after a long regular season and the playoffs at which point most hockey writers only wanted to take some well-deserved time off, it was a time of excitement and anticipation for young hockey hopefuls. Because most NHL players don't follow the same route of playing in college before turning pro as do the majority of their counterparts in baseball, basketball and football, it is not unreasonable for a handful of draft picks to make NHL rosters at the age of 18. These players are known by the time they are 14 or 15 and scouted heavily by the time they are 16 as they play for junior hockey teams throughout Canada, the U.S. and now, throughout Europe and beyond.

It is equally a day of hope for the NHL teams, as scouts and general managers dream of finding a couple of stars who can turn their franchise around sooner rather than later.

But it is a long day. A very long day, always at an NHL arena set up to accommodate the day's business.

At the start, there is the anticipatory a buzz of excitement, as team scouts, management and coaches fill the seats around the tables set up on the arena floor and review their wish lists of players. Deals are discussed with other teams; bargaining and persuasion are at a premium. It's like the stock market but with young, hockey-playing humans as the commodity. In the arena seating area are hundreds of draft hopefuls with their families, girlfriends, childhood friends, neighbors – all wanting to be there to witness this landmark day in the life of their 18-year-old son, brother, friend. During the time I covered the NHL, the draft was held on one day and consisted of 12 rounds, lasting into the early evening.

In the early rounds, young men would jump up out of their seats as their names were called, receiving a round of congratulatory hugs and handshakes before coming down to meet their new team. They would then don a jersey and baseball cap with their new team logo emblazoned on it, shaking hands with all of the execs surrounding the table of the team that now owned them. As the hours passed, the young men sitting in the arena seats would begin to slouch a bit. They would loosen their neckties, and their once-hopeful faces slacked with the beginnings of disappointment. If they were drafted in the later rounds, their expressions took on an "Oh God, thank you for saving me from the drive home without being drafted" look.

Every few years the draft buzzes with extra excitement, when a potential franchise player becomes available. Everyone knows it too, especially that "golden child" player. These are the shoo-ins, the players who know teams are whispering with each other, offering the world to have a chance to move up in the draft order to get a shot at selecting them. In the era when I covered the NHL there was no greater anticipation than in 1991 when phenom Eric Lindros, a power forward with strength, skill and burning competitiveness was lining up for the draft. Unlike Steve Yzerman (the Wings' top pick in 1983) or other highly touted draft-eligible players such as Joe Murphy or Jimmy Carson, Lindros came with rock star status and had his own PR machine. It was called Bonnie Lindros, mother to the 6'4" star of junior hockey. The Lindros family lived in London, Ontario, about halfway between Detroit and Toronto – maybe a two hour drive from either locale. As a result, Toronto and Detroit were the Lindros media hubs leading up to the 1991 Entry Draft.

To provide the Detroit media with an opportunity to interview Lindros before the draft, a press gathering was held at the Compuware Arena in Plymouth, due to Lindros' ties with the Compuware hockey program. As the NHL beat writer from *The Detroit News*, I received an invite to attend. This sort of press gathering was certainly out of the norm for hockey, though it is a common practice in other major sports. Its purpose is to give writers an opportunity to meet potential top picks in an informal setting, get their backstory and develop a relationship that could carry on after the player was selected.

Upon arriving at the Compuware Arena, I began hearing chatter about Bonnie, a powerful woman who acted as part agent, part guardian for her son. No one was going to take advantage of Eric under her watch. I could tell the media members were put off by the gall of this woman to interfere in her son's life. But now that I'm the mother of a teenage boy, I can understand. She was protecting her son's interest, and there was an awful lot at stake.

The real drama of the whole Lindros draft was not the anticipation of whether he would go first overall in the draft, but if the Quebec Nordiques – owners of the first pick – would have the guts to select him. Lindros and his PR/Marketing team (Bonnie) along with his agent (father, Carl) were very outspoken and clear that their son would not play for the Nordiques. The issues, from their perspective, were that Quebec City was a small market, the team wasn't good and Lindros deserved to play in a city that could appreciate his inevitable stardom. It was a bold move for a young player who hadn't yet placed one blade onto the ice in an NHL game.

So, naturally, as the media gathered around Eric at this press conference, most of the questions were about his reasoning for this decision and if he would follow through on the threat of not showing up for training camp if he did, indeed, get drafted by Quebec. Many of the reporters took the stance that Lindros was a spoiled, catered-to young man who would have to learn that he was not above the game. It was a valid point. Others – not many – applauded his individualistic approach and fortitude. I was somewhere in the middle. I figured, if you have enough talent to dictate where you want to work, go for it. But I am also not a fan of entitlement and all the posturing that goes with it.

After about 20 minutes of interviewing Lindros in a group media huddle, I zoned out. I started looking around the room, observing those in attendance before turning my attention back to Lindros as he held court. You can often learn more about a person through their actions and body language than you can from their words. Lindros was dressed impeccably in a suit that probably cost more than most items in my wardrobe combined. His shirt was pressed and his necktie wasn't even a fraction askew. He's one of those guys who looks just as comfortable in a suit and tie as he does in skates, pads and a jersey.

Then I looked closer at his necktie. It appeared to contain a multitude of family crests. That would be fitting, I thought. Or maybe the tie was from a country club or some other type of exclusive members-only society. Then I looked really close and nearly gasped when I realized what they were.

"Eric, is that what I think it is on your tie?" I asked.

Lindros' face lit up and he put on a mischievous smile. "What do you think it is?" he said, playfully.

"OK, are those all jock straps?" I boldly asked.

For the first time that afternoon Lindros seemed like the 18-year-old kid that he was. He started laughing but managed one final comment about it.

"You are the only one who noticed!" he said.

Later he gave me his home phone number in case I needed to

follow up with any other questions. I did have a question a few hours later and dialed the number. Bonnie answered.

"Hello, this is Cyndy Lambert. I was at the press conference today and I had a follow-up question for Eric. Is he available?"

"No, he is not," Bonnie said, sharply, then she paused. "Wait. Who did you say this was?"

"Cyndy Lambert. I'm with *The Detroit News*," I replied.

"Ah!" came her reply. "Were you the one who noticed his tie?"

I didn't know whether to laugh or become defensive. I went with the former.

"Yes. Yes I did," I said, allowing a slight chuckle.

"Eric told me as soon as he got home," she said. "I think that is just perfect. Leave it to the only woman in the room to pay attention."

"I thought it was pretty funny," I replied.

"Listen honey, Eric isn't home now but I'll have him call you back. I promise. In fact, any time you need to get ahold of him, you just call."

Because of simply noticing her son's necktie, I earned entry onto the Bonnie-approved short list of reporters who could interview Eric whenever I wanted. Bonnie gave me the family's other phone numbers and encouraged me to call whenever I wanted to talk to Eric, her or Carl. It was certainly the most surreal day of my career as I claimed success because I noticed artfully placed jock strap images on a necktie. But more interestingly for me, on a personal level, was that my individuality as a female reporter was recognized by someone else in a positive sense. And it wasn't noticed by just anyone, but by another woman. The fact that it was the mother of a future NHL Hall of Famer made it even more of a kick for me.

I'm sure there were countless other times during my career when the "guys" in the media had the angle because of their gender. But this time I had the advantage. And it sure felt good.

Fight Club

Cynthia Lambert

I'm not exactly sure where my love of hockey fights came from, but boy do I love them. As a reporter I took great pleasure in anticipating them, watching them, talking to the fighters, er, players, about their reasoning and strategy. And, of course, I loved writing about them. It was my editor Phil's idea to create a Tale of the Tape before one of the many anticipated fight "rematches" involving Bob Probert, Joe Kocur or whoever else was guarding the ice for the Wings against an anticipated foe. A Tale of the Tape is how the boxing world assesses an upcoming bout, noting the record, reach and other physical aspects of the boxers. At Phil's insistence, I did this for hockey fights. It was sheer brilliance!

Covering the Red Wings during what was referred to as the "Chuck" Norris days (the Wings were in the Norris Division), there were plenty of fights on the card in most games. The Wings were set with Bob Probert, Joe Kocur, Darren McCarty, Stu "The Grim Reaper" Grimson and Kevin McClelland on their roster at various times. While there were many great battles, a few stand out in my mind as the most notable. Here they are:

- *Scariest fight: Joe Kocur vs. Jim Kyte. Kyte was the first legally deaf player in the NHL. During a November game in 1988 between the Wings and Kyte's Winnipeg Jets, Kocur and Kyte tangled in a brief brawl with scary results. It began as a scuffle but within seconds Kocur landed a booming right to Kyte's head, knocking off his helmet and, some say, the hearing aid from his ear. Kocur then landed another right square to the side of Kyte's unprotected head. As Kyte crumbled to the ice, Kocur landed still another. Kocur was escorted off the ice by the linesmen, but Kyte remained in a heap on the ice, too stunned and injured to move. Teammates* helped the big player up, but as he skated off, he seemed to lose consciousness and fell to the ice again. The concussion Kyte suffered was one of the worst I ever witnessed. It also showed the power of Kocur's right – arguably the hardest punch ever in the NHL.

- **Prize fight:** Bob Probert vs. Tie Domi. It was February 9, 1992 and the New York Rangers' hard-headed (I mean, literally, this guy could take hard punches and act like they were feather slaps) enforcer Tie Domi wanted Bob Probert bad. It was being billed as the heavyweight championship of the NHL. Standing at 6'3", Probert towered over the 5'8" Domi. But that didn't stop the diminutive tough guy from chattering on about taking the NHL "heavyweight belt" from Probert. Fortunately for me and other members of the media, the fight took place at Madison Square Garden. I say lucky because the press seating at Madison Square Garden is in the lower level, nestled in the stands with the fans. As anticipated, Probert and Domi dropped their gloves and the fight ensued. During the lengthy fight, the two circled, wrestled and punched their way directly in front of the press box. The brawl was scrappy and had no clear winner. But because he held his own against the NHL fight champ Probert, Domi christened himself with the win. He did this by mimicking putting on the "heavyweight belt" as the linesman led him to the penalty box. This showboating stuck in the craw of other Red Wings and soon more fights started, creating a fight undercard of sorts, as some of the less "talented" fighters slugged it out to the delight of the crowd at the Garden. It was a grand night of anticipated brawling that did not disappoint.

- **Retribution:** Darren McCarty vs. Claude Lemieux. There are fights that are simply inevitable. One fight of destiny that has already gone down in history as one of the most *anticipated and notable – not to mention the one that breached all conventions of what hockey fights should look like and who they should include – came on March 26, 1997. This is when Detroit's Darren McCarty did what the whole Detroit team and many fans believed had to be done. McCarty sought retribution for Colorado Avalanche forward Claude Lemieux's dirty hit on Wings forward Kris Draper during the 1996 playoffs the previous spring. That hit from behind and into the boards left Draper with multiple facial fractures. Making matters worse for the Wings and their fans, the Avalanche, with Lemieux leading the way, went on to win the Stanley Cup that year. The next season the Wings were forced to wait for their payback as Lemieux sat out the first three games against Detroit. But he was in the lineup at Joe Louis Arena for that March game. As soon as they were on the ice together, McCarty took Lemieux to task, slugging the forward repeatedly with everything he had. Lemieux covered his head and fell to the ice, mimicking how you're supposed to defend yourself during a bear attack. Others, such as CBC-TV commentator and former NHL Coach Don Cherry, called it turtling. The Joe Louis Arena crowd was out of its collective mind with excitement over this scenic retribution. But it got even more interesting, as players began to pair off on the ice for multiple fights. The most astounding, though, was when Av's goalie Patrick Roy left the net to get involved. Wings goalie Mike Vernon who stood at 5'9" to Roy at 6'2", would have none of that and skated across the ice to tangle with the big goalie. There were so many fights going on simultaneously it was hard to decide what to watch. But, in the end, the blood-thirsty Wings and the more than 20,000 fans at Joe Louis Arena got what they wanted. And I was left with the task of trying to write a game story that said very little about the game, which was won in dramatic fashion by Detroit 6-5 in overtime, but instead offered great detail on the nuances of the brawls. It was my favorite regular season hockey game to cover … ever.*

It was 1965 and our family had just discovered Clark Lake, near Brooklyn, Michigan. I am holding my Grandma (Ida) St. Croix's hand on the dock, while my three brothers, Jerry, Steve and John, goof around in a row boat. We never stopped taking vacations here, and now Steve and his wife, Lauri, have a home right on Clark Lake.

Christmas at my grandparents' house on State Fair in Detroit. Here I am with my Grandpa (Dan) St. Croix and brothers Steve, Jerry and John.

83

My oldest nephew, Jeffrey, was the first to take in a Red Wings practice with me.

Because the Wings lost in the first round of the 1991 playoffs, I was able to join my parents in Maui for my cousin, Derrick's wedding to his sweetheart Danita.

Shortly after my mother passed, my dad, Jerry, attended a Red Wings practice with my brothers John and Steve – and their children – John's son Joe, and Steve's daughter Danielle and son Bret.

This was taken about one second after the jumpmaster pushed off to start the "dive" portion of my first-person story on skydiving. It is evident that I am positively terrified, yet, for the jumpmaster it's just another day at the office. *Photo credit: Dale Young/The Detroit News*

After freefalling for about 3,500 feet, I could finally breathe as we drifted down to the ground in the 9-cell chute. It took several minutes after we landed before I could stand on my wobbly legs. *Photo credit: Dale Young/ The Detroit News*

Through the years I was asked to write several magazine articles about the Wings star players, and was even part of an article about women sports writers (that's me with coach Jacques Demers in the photo on the right). I also collected many press passes, some of which are here. *Photo credit: Dale Pegg*

My most prized "collectible" possession: a Viacheslav Fetisov game jersey signed by the Russian Five – Fetisov, Igor Larionov, Sergei Fedorov, Vladimir Konstantinov and Vyacheslav Kozlov. *Photo credit: Dale Pegg*

Every fall, a week or so before training camp, the Red Wings traveled around Michigan on a press tour to promote hand-selected players and the upcoming season. Writers from Detroit who covered the team as their beat were invited to ride along. After a morning and early afternoon of press conferences the activity of choice was golf. Here I am flanked by (left to right) then-Wings PR manager Howard Berlin, longtime and legendary radio play-by-play man Bruce Martyn, player Keith Primeau and Wings sales representative Tony Nagorsen.

One of the kindest men I've ever met – former Wings PR Director Bill Jamieson.

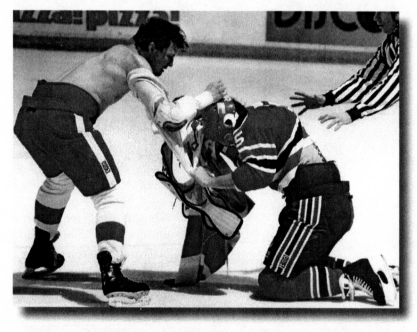

Bob Probert, one of the toughest players in NHL history, in one of his epic fights against New Jersey's Troy Crowder on January 28, 1991. *Photo credit: The Detroit News*

Darren McCarty exacts much-anticipated retribution – hockey style – on Colorado's Claude Lemieux on March 26, 1997. It is a payback for Lemieux's blindside hit on Wings forward Kris Draper the year before, which resulted in multiple facial fractures to Draper. *Photo credit: Alan Lessig/The Detroit News*

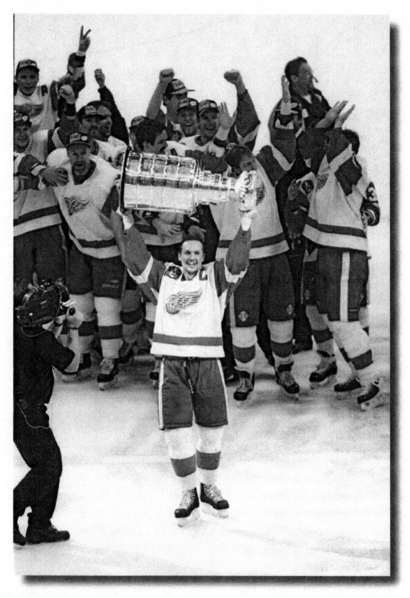

Red Wings captain Steve Yzerman hoists the Stanley Cup in celebration of Detroit's sweep of the Philadelphia Flyers in the Finals on June 7, 1997. *Photo credit: David Guralnick/The Detroit News*

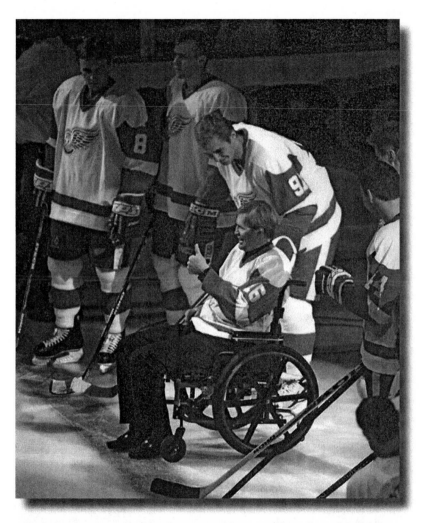

A little over a year after the devastating limousine accident that left him with extensive brain injuries, Wings defenseman Vladimir Konstantinov appears before the crowd at Joe Louis Arena before the Detroit's home-opener against St. Louis. *Photo credit: David Guralnick/The Detroit News*

After leaving my job at *The Detroit News* in 1998, I went to work for NHL team owner Peter Karmanos, Jr. at the company he cofounded: Compuware. And in 2006, his Carolina Hurricanes won the Stanley Cup. Here I am kissing the Cup with my five-year-old son, Quinn, who couldn't stop laughing.

9

Understanding Jacques

Being a good listener is an essential skill for a reporter, particularly when trying to figure out what is happening behind the scenes or what an exhausted athlete is trying to say between gasps of air.

Even more challenging is trying to see and decipher the truth between the shadows. And by shadows I mean the hints, the omissions of words or the blatant lies. In the hockey world these were usually generated by coaches and team management. But every so often the hockey world produced a coach or manager who was mostly honest, unique and a heck of a lot of fun. The kind of person where each day was an adventure in "what will he do, and what will he say?"

The first Red Wings coach I worked with as a full-time reporter was Jacques Demers. He was one of those guys. Jacques wouldn't exactly lie. Instead, he would dance around the truth when he wanted so badly to say something but knew he couldn't due to the delicate nature of potential trades or contract negotiations.

The heavens couldn't have picked a better coach for me to work with as a rookie reporter – and as a woman. He was completely accepting of me right from the start. I actually think he thought it was pretty cool that he got to work with one of the few female reporters in the NHL. I also felt a cool kind of bond with him, as if we had been friends in some alternate universe somewhere along the way. We understood each other and enjoyed each other's company.

I admired Jacques' passion for the sport of hockey and his generous heart. He is a kind and sensitive person who is unafraid of expressing his emotions – attributes that created a never-ending stream of quotable quotes and hilarious scenarios.

Here are some of the Jacques Demers gems I was privileged to witness in my years covering the team with him at the helm.

Some hockey fans may remember the game against the Minnesota North Stars during the 1987-88 season when Jacques and Stars Coach Herb Brooks got into a shouting match over a botched line change, dirty play or some other nastiness that had gone unpunished by the game officials. Jacques crawled down the bench to get closer to Brooks, who was equally enraged standing on the visitors' bench. Only a couple of panes of Plexiglas and a few feet separated the two.

As they shouted insults back and forth, one of the North Stars players or assistant coaches called out to Jacques: "You're nothing but a milk truck driver!" Always quick on his feet, Jacques retorted with a correction: "It was a Coca-Cola truck, it was a Coca-Cola truck!" (As a teen, Jacques drove a truck for Coca-Cola, a job he considered part of his interesting legacy.)

As the verbal assault continued between the coaches, it escalated as players got into the act by exchanging verbal jousts, while also pushing and shoving on the ice. Jacques, now fully enraged and engaged, grabbed the helmet of Wings player Tim Higgins, who was sitting on the bench in front of him. Jacques wanted to throw the helmet at Brooks. But when he tried to grab it, there was a tactical problem. Higgins had never detached the strap holding the helmet onto his head. As Jacques pulled on the helmet, Higgins made odd gurgling sounds. The result was a comical scene that made headlines across the NHL.

Higgins described the scene after the game in very simple terms.

"I kept trying to say to Jacques, 'It's still attached! It's still attached!'" Higgins said.

Fans loved Jacques' emotional approach to the game, especially considering the fact that the Red Wings were trying to climb their way out of the NHL cellar, where they had dwelled after a disastrous 1985-86 season. While Jacques was criticized by some for not having exceptional tactical skills for the game, his ability to motivate his players made up for his strategic shortcomings.

But even then, there were times when Jacques' attempts at motivation fell a bit short, leaving his players shaking their heads, confused by the intent of the message. One example came during what could be referred to as the dog days of the season – February or March. The team was on the road, in the middle of a long swing through western Canada. When the players came off the ice after practice, Jacques closed the dressing room door, leaving out all extraneous people (read: reporters) and delivered a much-needed motivational speech. As the media waited outside the dressing room, all that could be heard from inside the locker room were the muffled tones of the coach's voice. This went on for a couple of minutes when it was suddenly interrupted by a burst of laughter from the players.

Soon after the joyous outburst, the doors opened and a rejuvenated team exited. Jacques followed, laughing and wiping away tears from his reddened face.

"Cynthia," he said, which actually came out sounding like Cynsia, "I can't believe what I just said." Once he stopped laughing, he told me the story.

"I was talking with the players, telling them that these are the dog days of the season. I told them this is the time that separates the men from the boys. I kept going on and on about how they need to focus, to work hard … that we need them to be men, not boys."

"OK," I said, not following why this was so funny.

"I had them right there," he said, extending his arm and curling up his hand into a fist. "They were nodding their heads. Then I clapped my hands and said, 'OK boys, let's go!' Stevie (Yzerman) looked at me and just started laughing. Then I realized what I just said. My whole speech … gone! They were all laughing at me."

There were countless more stories about Jacques, his humor, his passion for the game, his kindness to others. But there also were those times when his French-Canadian roots shone through and created unintended humorous quotes along with a bit of confusion.

One night, star defenseman Darren Veitch didn't dress for the game. No reason for the sidelining was given. No one in the press box had a clue why Veitch wasn't playing, nor did Wings PR guy Bill Jamieson. After the game I asked Jacques why Veitch didn't dress.

"It was his tie," he snapped.

"His tie?" I replied to confirm this odd reason for keeping a star out of the game. Many possibilities swirled around my brain. Did Veitch not wear a tie on the team bus, which was part of the mandatory dress code? Did he wear a tie that was objectionable? What the hell could be the issue with his tie?

"Yes, Cyndy, his tie," Jacques repeated. "It's his right tie … he pulled a muscle in his right tie."

Ah yes, translated from his French-Canadian accent, that meant THIGH!

Meanwhile Demers looked at me as if I had suddenly developed some sort of learning disorder. When I told him what I thought he meant, we shared one of our many laughs.

Another one of my favorite Jacques-isms came as a trading deadline loomed. I don't recall what rumor I was chasing, but it was a good one – almost a certainty. Yet, every time I asked Jacques about it, he replied with a resounding, "No."

Before the next game I dared to ask again, at the urging of my editor, who also heard the same rumors of a pending trade. This time Jacques laid out his answer in plain English … or, rather, French.

"Cyndy, I've answered this question a dozen times. The answer is still the same as it's always been … NO! … N-O-N … NO!"

It was my favorite Jacques quote of my career.

Comic Relief
Cynthia Lambert

There are certain people in this world who look serious. Like, all the time. Sometimes it's how they act, other times it's the chiseled features that don't allow them to change their expression no matter what. Add in a ruthless work ethic and this is not the kind of person who one would think of as a joke-teller.

This was my initial reaction to Wings defenseman and former Soviet Red Army captain and warrior Vladimir Konstantinov. Konstantinov, through no fault of his own, was not what you would call "approachable." First, there was the language barrier when he first came to Detroit from Russia in 1991. Though his English progressed far faster than my Russian, he was still stoic and an unknown quantity to me for a couple of years, though I could sense a softness underneath his reserved nature. I admired him and loved his gritty game.

During the 1996-97 season, and after a loss against Chicago at the historic Chicago Stadium, the players loaded the bus for the ride back to the Drake Hotel. Because of the dicey neighborhood surrounding the stadium, it was often hard to get a cab after the game. I made it a practice to hitch a ride on the team bus immediately after the game, doing my writing in the comfort and safety of the hotel room.

The front few rows of the bus were reserved for the coaches, scouts and GM. The next couple of rows were for reporters, leaving the rest of the bus to the players. I swung into my seat on the right side, about three rows back and began to go over the game summary sheet that detailed shots on goal, minutes played and every other possible statistic on the game and each player. Upon entering, Konstantinov stopped at my row, looking at me. He was blocking the aisle way and holding up the rest of the team. He stared down at me. Finally, he spoke.

"Cyndy, let me see the shit," he ordered.

"The what?" I responded.

"You know, the shit. The shit about the game," he said, pointing to

the paper in my hands.

"Oh, you mean this?" I said, holding up the paper filled with statistics.

"Yeah," he said.

"Vlady, this is called a sheet," I said, over-pronouncing the word "sheet" to help him in his ongoing learning of the English language.

He took the paper from my hand, looked it over briefly, shook his head and handed it back to me.

"No Cyndy," he said. "This is SHIT!"

He allowed a whimsical smile, then retreated to the back of the bus, where he would sit and quietly listen to his teammates. It took several minutes before I could stop giggling about underestimating Vlady's comprehension of the English language and his sense of humor.

10

Kirk Gibson Isn't So Tough

Any female sports writer working in the industry in the 1980s knew about the reputation of certain athletes who, to be kind, didn't have an appreciation for women covering sports. The issue these men had wasn't necessarily that a woman was reporting on sports, but, instead, that she had the audacity to enter the locker room. The fact that nearly all interviewing of athletes is conducted in the locker room did little to persuade these athletes to understand the necessity of equal access.

In Detroit, this athlete was the Tigers' Kirk Gibson, better known as Gibby. A favorite son of the area, Gibson was born in Pontiac, Michigan, played football and baseball at Michigan State University and was selected by the Detroit Tigers in the first round of the amateur draft in 1978. He was revered for his competitiveness, talent and grit. Kirk was also powerful, good looking and personable.

Kirk and then-*Detroit News* sports reporter Lisa Dillman, who, like me, was also in her 20s, had several tumultuous encounters during the mid-80s. I would hear about these at the office, but didn't pay too much attention to them. I was just starting out in the business and didn't feel it was my place to ask too many questions or take sides. At that point, I had a very short list of negative encounters with athletes. There was the innocent slapstick run-in with rookie Shawn Burr and the particularly nasty encounter with Tiger Williams. I suppose my hope was that the time period of contesting a woman's place in the field of sports reporting had passed and we could all go on with our lives, working together as harmoniously as possible.

But that wasn't the case for Lisa and Kirk. And, truth be told, I was surprised at my own level of apathy regarding the situation and my reluctance to jump on the "Gibson is a jerk because he was mean to Lisa" bandwagon. Part of that was because I had enough on my plate. I didn't feel as though I needed to fight or even actively sympathize with anyone else's battles. What did I know? I hadn't yet experienced enough to have my opinion or empathy matter much. So I gave the cursory, "That's too bad; I hope it works out for you," reply to Lisa and kept my head down.

I also knew I was incredibly fortunate to be covering hockey. Countless times I told people about the politeness of NHL players, coaches, managers and scouts – not just the Red Wings but those from NHL organizations around the league. Even the players known for being challenging or surly seemed to accept me and gave me no problems. I knew I had it made with the sport I covered because of this. But there was another factor influencing my reluctance to become engaged in someone else's fight. I could only control my world and my relationships with anyone I covered. I didn't want to waste energy on a fight that wasn't personally mine, or in one where I didn't know all of the details.

I also think that my reluctance had something to do with the tolerance I learned growing up with three brothers. My brothers – Jerry, John and Steve – constantly had friends over to the house, so I learned very early how to navigate the waters of testosterone – in many cases not well, but I learned. My ego told me that I could work with any male athlete in a realm of respect and without prejudice. I didn't understand how others could have trouble with this. Yes, I was naïve in many ways, but at that point of my career, it worked to my advantage.

Fast forward to 1990. Kirk was now playing for the Los Angeles Dodgers and Detroit-area born hockey sensation Jimmy Carson had just been traded from the Edmonton Oilers to the Red Wings. Because of Carson's ties to the Detroit area – and the fact that the Wings could have and should have drafted him with their first selection in the 1986 entry draft instead of Joe Murphy (Carson was picked second by the L.A. Kings) – it was a fairly significant time to be an NHL/Red Wings reporter.

The Wings had just finished a West Coast road trip, finishing in Los Angeles. The team flew back immediately after the game the night before on their private jet. I stayed the night at my aunt and uncle's house in Glendale, and caught a flight the next day. As I walked through LAX, I noticed someone out of the corner of my eye. This person seemed to be looking at me, almost assessing me. I could see that the person was tall, likely a man, but I didn't want to make eye contact. Still, I could sense he was trying to keep pace with me. Finally, my curiosity got the best of me and I looked. It was Kirk Gibson, matching my strides about 10 feet to my left.

"Hey!" he half-shouted. "Are you Cynthia Lambert?"

"Oh no," I thought, bracing for a verbal assault. Instead, I gave a half smile and said, "Yes I am. Hi Kirk."

Kirk and I both stopped. He began looking around the area. I had no idea what was going to come next. Was he looking to see how many people would witness him yelling at me about being a sports reporter?

Instead, he had a question.

"Is Jimmy here? Jimmy Carson. Is he here?" Kirk asked. He looked like a little kid who was excited and anxious to see his long-lost friend. I informed him that Carson and the rest of the Red Wings team flew back the night before on the Wings private plane, Redbird One. I was about to continue walking to the gate when Gibby switched gears.

"How was the game last night?" he posed. There I was, in a busy corridor of Los Angeles International Airport talking hockey with Kirk Gibson. It was amusing to see passersby craning to see if it really was Gibby, and several approached him as we walked and chatted, seeking autographs. He complied, but kept talking to me, questions coming at a rapid-fire pace. He was desperate to talk hockey, the power play, playoff chances, trade rumors. We did this until we got to the gate. He, too, was heading back to Detroit.

Once we arrived at the gate, I got a bit nervous. Keep in mind that I was still in high school when Kirk was drafted by and began playing for the Tigers. In other words, I had been a big fan of his, and had swooned at him throughout my high school days whenever the Tigers were on TV. Now he wanted to talk with me! Kirk continued to ask questions and offer his opinions about the Wings. He asked about different players, the coaching, what I thought of different players in the league. The entire conversation blew my mind. This was Kirk Gibson. Why was he was being so freaking nice?

As I approached the gate, I took out my ticket to get my boarding pass from the gate agent. But Kirk grabbed it from me and said he'd take care of it. A few minutes later he handed me my boarding pass – I was now sitting in first class. It really was one of those moments that I couldn't wait to tell my mom about. She, too, was a big fan of Gibby.

On the plane, Kirk sat a couple of rows in back of me and across the aisle. I looked back once to thank him again for his kindness and he waved it off. No big deal. I glanced back one more time, feeling awkward that we weren't still talking, and he gave a little wave and grinned excitedly. It was just starting to hit me that he was actually happy that he ran into me, to talk hockey and get the scoop. And not once was he anything but a gentleman and, well, fun.

Periodically over the next few years I would run into Kirk in our shared neighborhood of Grosse Pointe or at games. One time, as I emerged from the Wings dressing room, he called me over. He wanted to introduce me to his wife, JoAnn. JoAnn was equally nice, and even encouraged me to stop by their house when I told her my typical walking path, which, unbeknownst to me, happened to pass their house.

Another time I was stopped at a light in Grosse Pointe, headed for a game at Joe Louis Arena. I heard a car horn honking next to me. When I looked, I saw it was Kirk, excitedly motioning for me to roll down my window. While waiting for the light to change, he extracted all the information he could from me about the Wings' playoff opponent and what I thought of their chances to advance to the next round.

It was at times like this that I was grateful I didn't enter into the fray of blaming or chastising someone with whom I had not had cross words with … just to support a colleague. Of course, if Lisa and I had been in a locker room together and I witnessed an athlete being disrespectful to her I would have certainly stepped in to defend her.

To this day I am grateful for what I consider to be a brief friendship with Gibby. And as I moved on in my career, I continued to remind myself to judge only on actions I experienced or witnessed. It was a great lesson learned … in a pretty cool way.

Life on the Road – the Good, the Bad and the Scary

Cynthia Lambert

There are certain perks you get to experience when you travel with a professional hockey team. Some of the best bonuses for me were the accommodations on the road. The team got amazing deals at four- and five-star hotels, and I happily rode on those coattails. Sometimes I was faced with the dilemma of whether to stay at the same hotel as the team or get my own room at a nearby Marriott, which has an amazing frequent stay program.

When I first signed up for the Marriott program it was at the franchise's hotel in Bloomington, Minnesota. Of all the Marriotts I've stayed in, this was the least plush, but it was only about mile from the airport and stood right across the street from the arena where the Minnesota North Stars played at the time. Because I didn't stay at Marriotts all of the time, I reasoned that perhaps within a year or two I would have enough points to stay a week for free somewhere nice. Little did I know how quickly I would accumulate these valued points.

That's because the Bloomington Marriott inadvertently credited my account with every hotel guest who came after me ... for one whole month. When I received my first Marriott statement I had accumulated 1,107,000 points. I could have traveled the world for free by redeeming all of them. But my honesty – and fear of opening up a whopping dose of bad karma – got the best of me. I called the 1-800 Marriott phone number and alerted them to this mistake. The agent was thankful for me bringing the error to her attention. She then proceeded to tell me I actually had 7,000 points – enough for nothing. It was a bit disappointing but I felt better about exposing the mistake.

Yet, when I got my statement the next month it was still wrong. The official statement erroneously showed a balance of 107,000 points – 100,000 more than I actually had. I placed another call to

Marriott, but this time it was to the conglomerate's redemption area. I booked a five-day stay in St. Thomas in the Virgin Islands with the bonus 100,000 points. I know it wasn't the truthful thing to do, but I thought my one attempt to right the situation was plenty. And besides, I needed a vacation.

Overall, my top two NHL-city hotels were in Chicago and Vancouver. The Drake in Chicago was filled with old-time opulence and class. In the late '80s the Drake still had white-gloved elevator operators who politely asked for your floor so they could transport you there. At the back wall of the elevator was a bench to allow for even more respite before entering the incredibly comfortable and well-appointed rooms. Many of what I would presume to be the original features of the historic hotel were still intact in the bathrooms and even the closets inside the room. My favorite time to stay at the Drake was during the Christmas season. The decorations were superb, right down to the huge and beautifully decorated tree in the lobby.

As wonderful as the Drake was, it couldn't compare to the total package of the Bayshore Westin in Vancouver. Situated on the banks of the ocean, with dense green pine trees lining the hills and mountains around it, the Bayshore's rooms were spacious and – the best feature – they had sliding door-walls. Opening that floor-to-ceiling door welcomed in the sound of the bay – the calls of the seagulls, the lapping of the water – and the amazingly aromatic air of the North Pacific. Getting to Vancouver was usually a lengthy ordeal so by the time I got to the room all I wanted to do was open that door-wall, pull a chair over to it and gaze out at the beauty of Vancouver. Even better was when the team built in extra time in Vancouver, giving me a chance to explore the city. My favorite activity was walking the long, swaying Capilano Suspension Bridge, located in North Vancouver. I could spend hours walking back and forth on the swaying bridge held together by wood and rope, hiking in the park at the other end of it, looking at the totem poles and breathing in the incredibly fresh air.

Perhaps third on my list – but with a disclaimer – is the Banff Springs Hotel, located in the picturesque ski resort area west of Calgary, Alberta. I stayed there, along with the team, for a couple of nights during the 1990-91 season when the schedule offered a couple-day gap between games in Calgary and Edmonton.

The hotel was built to resemble the architecture of a castle, adding to its mystique and lure. But you know what castles have? Towers and turrets. And turrets are round. The hotel designers then divided these into hotel rooms. When I opened the door of my room I saw a pie-shaped configuration with a twin bed, nightstand and tiny desk with a small television sitting atop it. The bathroom was also small, allowing just enough room for a toilet, sink, tiny shower and small rack for towels.

Adding to the drama and potential discomfort of the hotel were the rumors of its hauntings. Usually this sort of thing excited me, but not this time. The hotel was creepy. Lore says that, to this day, there are several ghosts that haunt its lobby, dining rooms, hallways and some guest rooms. And since the book I brought to read during my downtime was Stephen King's The Shining, *my spook factor was in overdrive. In fact, the hotel strongly resembled the setting for the movie version of* The Shining.

Because we were so far north – and because it was the dead of winter – darkness came early, at about 4 o'clock in the afternoon. I had finished my work by about 6 o'clock so I flicked on the TV. Three channels. None of them showing anything remotely interesting. I picked up my book and started reading, but I began to get scared. No, terrified. That's how creepy the whole room was. So I called down to the front desk and asked about a local movie theater. Success! Banff's movie theatre, the Lux, was only a 10-minute walk from the hotel – through wooded areas and then into town ... in the dark. I decided walking through the mountain trails to get to the movie theater was worth the risk. Though, I have to admit, the prospect of getting lost was not far from my mind; it happened to me often and in locales more easily navigated. But the thought of spending another six waking hours in that tiny room gave me all the motivation and weird brand of courage I needed.

I took the elevator down to the lobby, where I saw Bruce Martyn, the legendary Wings radio play-by-play man.

"Going into town?" Bruce asked.

"Yes, you?" I replied, hopeful.

Bruce was going to meet his broadcast partner and former NHL player Paul Woods at a restaurant in town and invited me to walk with him. I breathed a sigh of relief and the two of us walked out the front door of the hotel. A near-full moon lighted our way as we traveled away from the hotel. The path was breathtaking, with snow blanketing the mountain and most of the trail. Tall fragrant trees lined the way, creating some of the freshest air I had ever inhaled. As we meandered our way down the mountain trail I became lost in our conversation, all fear and reservations leaving me. I was startled when Bruce held out his arm to block me.

"Hold very still," he said, tilting his head to the right, indicating for me to look.

Emerging from the woods were three sizeable elk with racks as wide as their bodies were long. Apparently, elk can become spooked fairly easily and are prone to attacking. Bruce and I stood very still as the three of them gracefully walked within feet of us, crossing the path and entering the wooded area on the opposite side. It was shaping up to be a remarkable evening.

I bid farewell to Bruce when we arrived at the restaurant and proceeded the next few blocks by myself to the movie theater, not knowing what was playing and, honestly, not caring. But I did care when I saw what was on the marquee: Silence of the Lambs. *Really?*

My saving grace was that I had already read the book, so I thought I could handle the tale of FBI agent Clarice Starling and monster Hannibal Lecter. But as nearly everyone knows by now, the movie took the terror of Anthony Hopkins' depiction of cannibal Hannibal

Lecter to a new and awful level. Emerging from the theater at around 10 p.m. I was paralyzed with fear. I flagged down a cab, told the driver where I needed to go and explained why I didn't want to walk the half mile to the hotel, as if I needed to tell him. But he nodded and laughed, saying he was glad he could help me out.

"Don't worry, I'll get you there safely," he promised.

I've not been back to the Banff Springs Hotel, but since binge-watching the TV show Supernatural *with my teen son, Quinn, who is now equally curious about spirits and ghosts, I think I might have to find my way back there one day. But maybe in the summer when it's light all day ... and most of the night.*

11

The Day That Wouldn't End

I have no sense of direction.

I am both amazed and baffled by people who can stand inside a building and casually say something like, "Oh, yeah. The Starbucks is five blocks north of here," then *point* in the direction that is north. How do they do that?

This has been a mystery to me for my entire life. And because of my lack of directional sense, I, unfortunately, have many stories of me trying to navigate my car, knowing I had to stick with my original directions regardless of delays or obstacles because if I deviated I could end up hundreds of miles away from my desired end point and no clue how to right the wrong. While I admire those who seem to have swallowed a compass, they have remained a mystery for my entire life, as has directional intuition.

Other than one year when I lived in the Los Angeles area as I contemplated my collegiate plan, I have always lived on the east side of Detroit, a mere 10 miles or so from downtown. I know of a handful of ways to navigate myself to prominent landmarks: Joe Louis Arena, Little Ceasars Arena, the Fisher Theatre, Comerica Park, Ford Field, Campus Martius Park, Belle Isle, Eastern Market,

Lafayette Coney Island or any other well-known destination within the city limits.

But my navigation issues don't just involve driving. My lack of direction is so bad I can go for a walk down a twisting/turning road in my own neighborhood and have absolutely no idea if I should turn left or right to get home. As a result, simple three-mile walks have turned into five-mile endurance treks ... just because I have no idea which direction I am heading after looping through a handful of subdivision streets.

Now picture me traveling all around North America covering the Red Wings. My early days of reporting on the team were fairly simple. I used the same travel agency – the one owned by former Red Wings player and longtime TV commentator Mickey Redmond. This way I could be booked on the same plane with the team. This also meant I could hop on the team bus from the airport to the hotel. Then came Red Bird One, the Wings' private team plane. Reporters were not allowed to ride along due to insurance considerations ... or at least that's the reason provided by the team. So from that point on I was on my own.

I would never rent a car on the road because of my navigational challenges. To do so would get me lost quicker anyway. And having no context for identifying landmarks in these NHL cities – and no GPS – to give me perspective, I figured it could potentially lead to tragedy. Ironically, the only city where I did rent a car was Los Angeles, likely the second most congested area to drive in after New York City. I did this because I knew L.A. well. After getting my Associates degree in business from Macomb Community College I thought my higher education path would take me to finance and economics. I had always wanted to live in California so when close family friends offered to board me at their home in the L.A. suburb of Glendale, I took the chance, figuring I could work for a year to establish my residency, then attend UCLA to get my Bachelor's degree. (Obviously, I changed my mind, switched majors and returned back to Detroit.) Regardless, during that year spent in southern California I learned how to navigate the complicated freeway system and was completely comfortable driving there ... especially because the freeways were always backed up, meaning I never went very fast, which gave me time to plan my route.

I have many, many stories of travel woes – delayed flights, cancelled flights, uncomfortable flights, prop plane flights where I could visibly see ice building up on the wings and flaps (this was Alberta in January with a ground temperature of -65 degrees Celsius), harrowing taxi cab rides, hotel rooms with loud in-room heating systems, missed flights due to extenuating circumstances and even one missed road trip to Long Island because I couldn't get my car out of my own driveway due to the frozen snow drifts piled behind it.

There was one awful trip, however, that will forever stick in my mind – a two-game swing in the late 1980s that first took the Wings to a neutral-site preseason game in Houston and then on to Toronto. This was before electronic plane tickets – at that point in time the internet was still just a dream in Al Gore's mind – so all of the information about the flight was crammed into one small rectangular document that *could not* be lost.

I arrived with the team in Houston, then traveled to the hotel on the team bus. One of the keys to effectively traveling with the Red Wings was to never check a bag. If I did, the team bus would be long gone by the time I retrieved my bag from the luggage carousel. I didn't want that. This meant I had to schlep an oversized carry-on bag containing my clothes on one shoulder (this was before the time of luggage with stable wheels). I would sling my laptop computer bag, which also contained all of my reference books, on my other shoulder. In those days laptops were not as slim and lightweight as they are today. My work computer at that time was at least 10-15 pounds. And, again, because the internet wasn't up and running yet, I crammed a number of reference materials in the laptop bag as well, including the large NHL Guide and Record Book, individual media guides for the teams the Wings were going to play and any other documents or papers I thought were necessary. As a result, the computer bag on my shoulder felt like a bag of rocks. Walking through the airport I could have been mistaken for a Sherpa or, on my less attractive days, a pack mule.

I had never before been to Houston. I knew its heat and humidity were legendary during the summer, but somehow in my mind, I figured Houston in September would mimic Detroit or Toronto in early fall. Big mistake. During the short walk from the airport to the team bus I nearly melted. I'm not sure if there was a heat wave hitting the city or if it was just business as usual with the weather but it was oppressive.

"Swell," I thought. "Which sweater should I wear to the game tonight?"

As it turned out, I was in luck. The hotel was actually connected to the arena. I wouldn't have to walk outside at all. It seemed that all was going my way. According to the team's itinerary, the players and coaches were meeting in the hotel lobby first then walking to the arena. I joined them, following through the intricate pathway that connected the hotel to the arena. As I followed along, I forced myself to notice landmarks – rose colored carpet, chrome and glass structure, long hallways with glass and chrome doors, a left at the kitchen, a right at the big conference room. Short of leaving a trail of bread, this was how I managed.

After the game ended, I conducted my interviews, put the final touches on my story and updated my notebook. Then I packed up and headed out of the press box, looking forward to settling back into my hotel room for a good, albeit, short rest before getting up to catch my flight to Toronto. I meandered my way through the corridor, saying hello to the passing custodian or arena worker as I looked for the door that connected the arena to the hotel. After one lap of the building I couldn't find it. I started to panic. Then I saw a group of men in suits walking out a door. Though I couldn't be sure, they looked like hockey players – young, athletic builds and wearing suits. I went with this theory and decided I should follow them, hoping they knew where the correct door was.

I followed at a safe distance so they wouldn't realize I was trailing them. When I went through the door they used as an exit I was greeted with the stifling heat of Houston. I was outside, not in the connecting hallway. No worries, I thought. I'll just follow them back to the hotel, naively thinking they were as boring as me and would want a good night's sleep. I soon realized they were branching out into the city streets of Houston, which, at that point in time, was one of the most dangerous cities in the U.S. I continued to follow, thinking I was somehow protected by the players striding along 50 paces ahead of me. Surely, if they heard me screaming from an attack they would turn back to help. Right?

Up ahead the group rounded a corner. I hustled to catch up, but when I turned the corner they were gone. I figured they must have entered the establishment down a few doors. With my plan in the dumpster at this point, I followed them in. As I entered the establishment I quickly realized this was certainly not the type of bar I would normally – or ever – frequent. Adding to the revelations of the evening, the men who bellied up to the bar were not Red Wings players, but middle-aged men in suits. I had just traveled a good half mile away from the arena for nothing.

I retreated to the streets and was immediately frightened ... and hot. It was now about midnight. And since it was a weekday there was not much foot traffic. I had no landmarks, no cell phone (this time period predated those, too) and was lugging my trusty 15-pound computer and reference guides. I was a sitting duck with a boulder dangling from my shoulder. So I just kept walking ... thinking, or rather hoping, I was heading back toward the arena.

Suddenly, across the street I saw the familiar chrome and glass of the hotel! I jaywalked across a desolate major street and made my way toward the building. A group of young men (in my midnight brain: a gang) approached me. Actually, maybe they were a gang. I walked as swiftly past them as I could, acting as if I couldn't hear what they were saying and muttering to myself the Catholic mantra I grew up with: "Sacred heart of Jesus, I place my trust in thee." I darted into the open ramp of the connected parking garage where lights shone brightly. The men didn't follow. As I made my way into the guts of the parking garage I saw a glass door with light blue carpeting, very similar in style to the rose colored carpeting of the hotel.

"This must be a different entrance point to the hotel," I reasoned.

I entered through the door and it closed silently behind me. At the far end were double doors of still more glass and chrome. When I tried them, they were locked. Ugh. To my right was an elevator.

"The hotel lobby must be on the second or third floor and I just didn't notice it when we checked in," I reasoned to myself.

I pushed the button and the doors opened immediately. Once inside, I didn't see the familiar L* for Lobby, just a long list of ascending numbers. I pressed 2, thinking that if I built this hotel I would put the lobby on the second floor. After the short ride up, the doors opened and I stepped out. Again, there were glass and chrome double doors to my right. I went to them but they wouldn't open. This time I saw a buzzer mounted to the wall, so I buzzed it.

"Hello?" said a woman's voice laced with a distinct south Texas drawl.

"Hi, I need to get through these doors and they're locked," I answered. "I'm on the second floor."

"Are you sure you want to do that, honey?" she asked.

Almost sure, I thought, but, "Yes," is what I replied.

She buzzed me in. Once beyond the doors I saw a long walkway to another set of double glass and chrome doors. I traveled the distance and tried them. Locked. I backtracked and returned to the original doors. Locked! As my sense of panic began to seep in, I took a moment to actually see where I was; to gain some sort of perspective. It was then I saw that I was in a glass tube with wall-to-wall powder blue carpet. The glass connector hung high above the deserted streets of Houston, giving those in it a view of the town and those on foot a chance to see who was walking through it. I felt like a hamster in its habitrail. After the long day and the stress of intuitively knowing I was going to get lost (and then proving myself right), getting trapped in this glass and chrome funhouse was more than I could handle. I threw my bags to the ground and began thoroughly and without editing, screaming at myself for being so stupid. I paced back and forth as I let loose with expletives that accurately described my pathetic nature at that moment. Then came the tears of frustration and fear – just a few to punctuate the evening's catastrophe. Not only was I trapped, but at this point it was late – nearly one in the morning. And my flight to Toronto was less than six hours away.

Then I saw it. A tiny buzzer by the door where I had come in. Salvation! I sprinted to it and buzzed it.

"Hello?" came the now familiar woman's voice.

"Hi, I thought I needed to be in here, but I was wrong. This isn't my hotel," I explained.

"Yeah, I didn't think so," she replied. "This building hasn't opened yet."

Well, this was unexpected news. I had talked my way into a building still under construction.

"Can you please let me out?" I asked.

"I sure can," she said, "but why don't I send a security guard over to you so you can make it back safely."

That brought me great relief. I thanked her and told her where I was staying so she could convey that to the security guard.

"We'll get you there; you're not far," she said. I'm not sure, but I thought I heard her chuckling.

"Well, OK," I said. "How long is it going to be? This is kind of scary; I feel like a fish in a bowl."

Then came her fated reply.

"Oh, don't you worry, I've got you on camera. I've been watching you the whole time."

You have got to be kidding me, was my first thought. Then I recalled what I had been doing – all of which she saw. My tantrum, pacing back and forth, yelling at myself. My utter mortification at the show I gave her was alleviated within 10 minutes when the security guard showed up and walked me back to my hotel. It took about three minutes. I was so close. Once I saw the hotel I asked the guard to peel off and let me take it from there, just in case anyone I knew saw me being escorted back. I didn't want to deal with any questions and be forced to tell their embarrassing answers. I fell into bed, praying to the God of Directions to please bestow me with some ... soon.

The next morning I took a cab to the airport. I don't recall why, but I had booked a different flight than the team. When I arrived at the airport I was told that my flight was leaving in 10 minutes. I had read the ticket wrong, mistaking the flight number for the flight time. Panic hit again, but this time the Houston airport personnel were on it. The American Airlines ticket agent called for a shuttle to whisk me to the correct terminal to maybe, just maybe, catch my flight. I felt like I was in some kind of suspense thriller movie. The shuttle met me at the curb and whisked me away, speeding along the circular road surrounding the airport. I disembarked the shuttle and ran to the gate where the agent was ready with a smile to take my ticket. Out of breath, I boarded the plane, all eyes on me as I played a human game of bumper pool with my luggage as I navigated my way down the narrow aisle. Some passengers smiled politely at me; many rolled their eyes my way. Apparently the flight had been held for me and some of my flight-mates weren't all too happy about it. But I didn't really care much at that point. I stored my luggage in the overhead bin, surprised that there was still room, and took my seat. Perspiration flooded out of my pores and relief permeated my very being. I made it!

As I continued to collect my wits and relax into my seat, I noticed we still weren't moving. Fifteen minutes later, we were still at the gate. Then came the announcement. Due to a mechanical issue, the flight was now cancelled. They weren't waiting for me after all.

After a series of ticket changes and more delays (that included a three-hour layover in Kansas City), I arrived in Toronto, completely exhausted physically, mentally and emotionally. It took more than nine hours to travel about 1,500 miles. My laptop battery died somewhere en route to Kansas City for my "convenient" connection, meaning I couldn't write my story and notebook due for the next day's paper. I would have to finish it when I got to the hotel. Making matters worse, I had guzzled way too many cups of coffee on the flights and ate very little food to counter the caffeine. By early evening when we landed I was in full rebound from the caffeine, feeling exhausted and shaky. Instead of doing the smart thing and packing all of my reference books into my carryon bag, I decided to carry them out in my arms, like some school girl on a college campus.

I emerged from the plane's jetway – where, in pre-9/11 days people meeting the passengers were allowed to congregate – with my laptop strap flung over one shoulder, the strap of my suitcase over the other and my hands cradling my reference books. I glanced at the happy and anticipatory faces before me, wishing more than anything that a loved one was there waiting for me. They would give me a hug, and then say something to the effect of, "Why are you carrying all this? Give me some of it." They would then take my books and one of my bags and whisk me away to a warm and comfortable house for a delicious home-cooked meal and a relaxing night of conversation.

But nothing remotely close to that happened. Instead, my foot caught on something and I began a momentous fall. My hands, full of books and notebooks, couldn't help me pull out of this new equilibrium issue so I continued to vault forward. Eventually, I landed on my hands and knees, books flying forward and ass in the air for all those behind me to see. Thank God I was wearing jeans and not a skirt, but still, the indignity of it all was too much for me to bear. I'll never forget the looks on the faces of the people pulled from their joy to witness this train wreck of a scene. Was it surprise? Confusion? Sympathy? Delight? I quickly accepted help from the total strangers who collected my books and asked if I was OK. I smiled, choking back tears fueled by exhaustion, embarrassment and too much caffeine, and limped off to still another taxi cab.

Once safely in my hotel room I collapsed on the bed and dialed my mom. As the story of my horrid day unfolded over the phone line, my mother wailed with laughter, calling to my dad in the next room so that she could tell him in real-time the hilarious travel story of my day. It was times like that I realized where I got my resilience ... and sense of humor.

Hold the Coffey

Cynthia Lambert

Despite earning a degree in broadcast journalism, there ended up being a multitude of reasons why I pursued a career in print rather than broadcast media, the primary reason because of the job I landed at The Detroit News *while I was still in college. It made complete sense for me to stick with newspaper work. And because of that, the world was saved from seeing and hearing the real me, the one who is a cross between journalist Cynthia Lambert and a poor woman's version of Carol Burnett ... and not on purpose.*

I tend to say things that are best left between me and my interviewee. I am prone to mixing up words when I talk, rambling on and on, dropping things, running into doorways and tripping over things like bunched up rugs or even twigs on the sidewalk. For the duration of my 14-year career I was grateful to be hidden behind the veil of pen and paper with minutes and sometimes hours to work on my articles and fix mistakes. This distance served me well, and, at least partially, kept my reputation as a professional intact. Never was I more grateful for this than when I was interviewing future Hall of Fame defenseman Paul Coffey over the phone from the privacy of my home office. This came during the fall of 1996 when Detroit was talking with the Hartford Whalers about trading Coffey and forward Keith Primeau for All-Star forward Brendan Shanahan. It was hard to get Coffey alone for an exclusive interview, so when my home phone rang and it was Coffey complying to my request for a one-on-one chat, I was beyond thrilled.

My home office consisted of bookcases, a desk and an upholstered chair on rollers with a square back and fixed wooden arm rests. The best feature was that the chair not only swiveled but it also rocked back and forth. For me, my whole office setup was warm and inviting, yet still serviceable. Even my phone was perfect for me — cordless so that I could walk around as I talked. When I answered the phone and discovered it was Coffey, I turned on my computer and settled both hands on the keyboard. All I had to do was ask him a couple of questions and he was off and running with great quotes. I held the phone receiver between my right shoulder and right ear, freeing up my hands to type away. Settling into the interview, I leaned back to relax a bit more as I fired off another question. But I leaned back just a smidge too much and my serviceable chair tipped backward with me in it, the phone still wedged between my ear and shoulder. I know I released some sort of panicked exclamation that probably sounded something like, "Whupadangcrudya." Fortunately for me, it must have sounded like an appropriate response to what Coffey had just said, because he kept on talking.

But my predicament had just begun.

There I was, flipped onto my back, feet in the air, phone suctioned to my ear and no computer, pen or notebook to record his answers. That was the worst part of it. Because of the wooden arm rests and the square back of the chair, I was stuck. I tried rolling out of the chair to the right, but the arm rest was too tall and wide for me to negotiate an exit without a struggle that I was sure would be audible. I tried wiggling the chair to roll it over. It wasn't budging.

This is the worst possible situation for a reporter on the verge of getting a scoop, or at least a quote that hadn't already circled around North America five times in dozens of newspapers. I couldn't jot down even a single note. The sheer buffoonery of what was happening did not escape me, either. I did my best to suppress the awkward and nervous kind of giggle, sort of like the kind you get in church. I held the phone away from my face so that Coffey couldn't hear me. This was an important strategy, as he was stating the reason why he believed he should stay in Detroit. He was making exceptional points, all of which I needed to commit to memory so that I could accurately paraphrase him after I managed to free myself.

After about 10 minutes into my predicament, the blood had rushed to my head and my legs were tingling and nearly numb. By that time we had, thank God, covered all of my questions. The interview was completed. I thanked him for his time, clicked off the phone and did a backward somersault out of my stylish chair. Then I wrote down everything I could remember, doing my best to stay focused when all I really wanted to do was laugh.

While that interview situation was the most awkward, there were many others that fell into the same embarrassing category. One occurred as I chatted with Minnesota North Stars franchise player Mike Modano, a Detroit-area native. Mike was very warm and welcoming, and we were enjoying a nice conversation in front of his stall in the visitors' dressing room at Joe Louis Arena. Seated to his left, I fired away questions and efficiently scribbled down his replies. Tucked inside my jacket pocket was my brand new Detroit News-*issued cell phone. Being early-1990s technology, the phone was big and clunky, and when I talked on it for more than 10 minutes it got really hot on my ear. I had silenced the ringer and set it on vibrate. But this was a different type of vibrate than, say, an iPhone would produce today. Instead, it created a vibration that felt more like one of those electronic disks you get at restaurants – the ones that buzz and vibrate when you're next up to be seated.*

Again, the fates were on my side because I don't think Modano ever knew what happened. I had asked him a question, to which he was in the process of replying with a passionate response. Just then, my phone rang – er, vibrated. It felt like an electrical jolt through my body. I uttered something that was a cross between a gasp and a scream, staring straight into Modano's eyes. Instead of stopping and asking what I was yelling about, his response was: "I know! Right?"

12

"No Bill, Just You"

By the early 1990s and with a number of years under my belt as the full-time Red Wings beat writer, life settled into a bit of a routine. It went something like this:

1. Get the Red Wings schedule sometime over the summer and chart out key games in the season, the All-Star break, long road trips, etc.
2. Pray that the trip to Buffalo was NOT part of a longer trip to New York City or New Jersey so I could beg off the Sabres game without missing out on all the fun in New York City.
3. Note the trips where friends or relatives might meet me on the road for a bit of fun.
4. See when the long road trip out west in March was scheduled so I could schedule vacation time and book a flight for my yearly 10-day stay in Maui to power up for the playoffs.

This is how a beat writer often thinks – in terms of road trips.

As I entered my fourth year on the beat, Jacques Demers remained coach of the Wings, I continued to build up my "sources" contact list and began to create a network of reporters in NHL cities around North America ... a crucial step in effectively "covering" the NHL. At that time, not many newspapers were online. That meant

I had to get all of my information from other hard copy newspapers, magazines or from conversations with reporters or team personnel.

To supplement my weekly around-the-NHL notes column, I called fellow writers to get information from their city – or what they had heard from other reporters. Information shared with me by other reporters I trusted was acceptable to include in my NHL column. This created a telephone line of sorts between reporters to help each other round out their weekly NHL columns. Most cities had at least two newspapers; and, therefore, at least two reporters. I inherited previous Wings beat writer Vartan Kupelian's contact list at the different papers around the league. This way I wasn't providing info to a contact in Chicago, for instance, who was also friendly with the reporter from the *Detroit Free Press*.

It didn't take me long to develop relationships with other reporters. The majority of NHL writers I dealt with were extremely helpful and supportive; I then modeled their behavior and dropped everything if one of them called, needing notes or information.

Filling the weekly notebook was also a great way to further develop reporter contacts in other NHL cities. We were, after all, quasi-colleagues. More often than not, I felt a stronger connection with writers who were hundreds or thousands of miles away from me than I did with those 10 miles away sitting in *The Detroit News* sports department.

This brings up the situation of the office. As a sports beat writer, your "office" is predominantly the arena, field, course or court. The colleagues you interact with most often are the beat writers in other cities. With hockey, most nights I was on my own at the Joe Louis Arena press box. This was the case for two main reasons. First, at that time, hockey, even in Detroit, was still considered the fourth major sport behind baseball, football and basketball. Second, the Wings weren't very good in the late 1980s and early 1990s. Every so often a columnist or sidebar writer would show up to offer another perspective on the Wings. When this happened, it seemed rather odd for me to have a fellow *News* writer to talk to or share information with. Most often I was the lone wolf in the three *Detroit News* seats in the press box. On occasion the other seats were taken by players who weren't in the lineup that night, scouts or other visitors. Legendary Detroit TV weather man Sonny Eliot often took one of the seats and filled gaps in action telling me silly jokes and stories. He was a delight.

Because my workplace was predominantly at the arena or on the road, I was told that my desk at *The News* was going to be given away to another sports reporter who needed it more. "Just work out of your house," my boss instructed me. This was like a gift from the gods. Work out of my house, go to practices and games, and travel for road games.

Life was pretty darned good.

Then came September 17, 1990. This is when several of the New England Patriots football players verbally and sexually abused Boston Herald reporter Lisa Olsen while she was attempting to interview one of their teammates in the locker room. I had only met Lisa briefly when she did some NHL feature reporting/writing on the Bruins. She was professional and seemed like a very nice person. But whether she was nice or not, she didn't deserve the treatment she received from the NFL "professional" athletes. What the players did and said was reported widely – they taunted her and made lude sexual gestures to unnerve her – painting a picture of privileged bullies trying to intimidate someone who was only trying to do her job. Or at least that's how I saw it.

It didn't take long for the sharks to start circling me. Fellow reporters who had never spoken to me before about how I ended up in my job were suddenly interested hearing from me what it was like to be a "female" sports reporter.

"How do you think it's different being a female reporter?" was the main question directed to me, followed closely by, "Do you think the players treat you differently because you're a woman?"

I'm sure most of my fellow reporters were asked (read: told) by their editors to see if the NHL had the same problem – athletes targeting women reporters. I understood their predicament, but it was annoying. It would be like all of a sudden asking an accountant if they thought their colleagues treat them differently because they're left handed. It's a comparative question, and unless you've ever experienced what it is like to be the opposite there is no way of knowing whether you are being treated differently.

So I came up with my pat answer – something I know every reporter disdains getting in response. I decided on: "I don't know; I've never been a male reporter."

This didn't go over so well. People wanted dirt. They wanted my battle stories of how Red Wings players mistreated me, how they were nasty to me, walked naked in front of me daring me to say something to them, snarled sexist jokes to me. But, thankfully, I had nothing. Other than a few isolated incidents, I didn't even have a sniff of a story to share. This was completely accepted by my NHL compatriots because they had been dealing with hockey players, coaches, scouts and officials just as I had. Generally speaking, the NHL-employed were a very decent – if not overly polite – lot.

Even my editors at *The News* pulled me aside to let me know they supported me and that I needed to come to them if any player, manager, coach or water boy caused me problems based solely on the fact that I was a woman. More to the point, they wanted to know if there were any lewd or sexist remarks directed toward me.

By this time, though, I had figured out how to navigate through any minor issues with my sources. More importantly, when I had conflicts with players, coaches, scouts or NHL officials, I never once felt that it was because I was a woman. In fact, I think the opposite happened. I believe the Wings players in particular, were a bit kinder to me than they were to my male counterparts. This, of course, could have been the result of the Red Wings team being led by captain Steve Yzerman. To say Steve epitomized the term class-act doesn't tell the whole story. He's a smart and talented man with a great understanding of people. In his playing days he always seemed to know how to handle reporters with professionalism, grace and boundaries. But if you crossed Steve, when he felt you were unfair, he would let you know by flashing his steely-eyed look. He would followed that up with very precise sentences regarding the issue. No mincing words, no passive aggressiveness. Only honesty. While I believe Steve influenced the temperament in the locker room, I also believe my lack of issues with players was reflective of the type of person who plays, coaches or manages professional hockey. During my career I had many conversations with other reporters about the similarities in hockey players' demeanor regardless of what team they played for or whether they hailed from Canada, the U.S., Sweden, Russia or any other locale. Hockey players, as a general rule, are polite people. Why this is the case is anyone's guess. But every hockey reporter has reaped the benefits of the overall accepting atmosphere surrounding hockey, especially when compared to other sports.

After about a week of the female sports reporter focus, I began to think the subject was dying down. But then a producer from Detroit's WXYZ-TV, Channel 7 contacted me. Lead news anchor Bill Bonds wanted to interview me about the "Lisa Olsen incident." It wasn't the New England Patriots incident, it was Lisa's. That should have been my clue how the interview was going to go.

I agreed to do the interview with some reluctance. Doing interviews with print reporters who were colleagues was one thing. But to go on local television with Detroit's most highly rated news anchor who made his name slicing and dicing his interviewees was quite another. I was not sure I could hold my own against Bonds. I was scared.

Another reason I didn't necessarily want to take this to another level was because of my feelings about feminism, as most people commonly think of it. I supported equality, but was not one to rage against the machine to get it. Perhaps I was fortunate that my path in a man's world seemed to open up before me with only limited challenges. Not all women are that lucky. My career choice was one I made consciously, knowing I would likely have to face barriers and prejudice. I encountered very few in the first category and just a few more in the second. Again, I was lucky. I simply loved sports and got a real kick out of being the first to report news. That's why my career was a good fit for me. I agreed to the interview with Bill Bonds because my boss thought it would be good press for *The News*. I was a good employee who was willing to take one for the team. I also felt it was important to stand up for myself as a reporter in Detroit.

So after covering that day's Red Wings practice, and writing my notes and article, I drove from my home to Channel 7's studios. This is where it started to get weird. While the newscast was going on, a production assistant set me up in an adjacent room that looked like a library of sorts. He provided me with an earpiece and a microphone clipped to my sky-blue jacket. The interview was going to be conducted "remotely." It was going to look like I was in my home or office instead of a few feet from where Bill Bonds actually sat. So there I was, waiting for the light on the camera in front of me to shine red so the verbal blood bath could begin.

As I waited, my trepidation about the interview grew. I knew Bonds was going to try his best to reel me in only to clobber me in the end with a dramatic statement to show his superiority, then have the feed cut off so that he could have the last word. It made for "great TV" and allowed him the opportunity to come off as a hardnosed journalist. He was already a legend in Detroit and I, still in the waxing years of my career, knew I was no match for him.

Finally, the light came on and the interview commenced. It lasted only about 90 seconds, but it seemed like a time warp – was I there for an hour or 10 seconds? For the most part Bonds asked typical questions – what's it like to be a female sports reporter ("I don't know. I've never been a male sports reporter"), what is Lisa Olsen like, do I think women should have equal access to the locker room, etc. Then his final series of questions began. I could sense him lining up for the kill. Without coming out and saying it, his questions were beginning to hint that I had voyeuristic motives for wanting to be a sports reporter; that the only reason I pursued this career was to go into locker rooms and see naked men. With each of his attempts, I was able to direct the question or innuendo away with a straightforward reply. With time running short, he cut to the chase.

"C'mon Cynthia. Don't all your friends ask you if Steve Yzerman has nice buns?"

There it was. That's what he wanted to ask all along. Without pausing, I heard myself say: "No Bill, just you."

Then I smiled and stopped talking. There was a slight pause, and Bonds started laughing. He thanked me for taking the time to chat with him. The red light went off on the camera and Bonds moved on to tease the next story.

I exhaled, disconnected the microphone, removed the earpiece and started to head out of the studio, eternally grateful that I hadn't embarrassed myself too badly. Before I got to the door, I was asked by someone working for the telecast to wait. Apparently, Bonds wanted to say something to me. I was directed to a phone on the wall. I picked up the receiver and gave a measured, "Hello?"

Bonds proceeded to thank me for being such a good sport and for creating "good TV." Sure. No problem.

On the drive home I pondered how I was able to come up with the retort to the "Yzerman buns" question so quickly. I am not usually that quick on my feet, and when I do respond quickly it's usually not succinct or brilliant in any way. This is why I am a writer, not a broadcaster. I decided that what happened was Divine intervention. My guardian angels were putting the words on my tongue. And thank God they did. To this day I'm glad my retort was playful and not snide because good old Bill Bonds would have shredded me on the spot.

Shortly after that interview, the hubbub died down. Interestingly, many of the Red Wings players were also being interviewed about their experiences working with me and other female reporters. I knew I had finally "made it" when many of them approached me afterward to say they were tired of that line of questioning. "She's just doing her damn job!" was the common response they gave. They also had the same question as me. Why is this such a big deal? It was then that I could actually sense the amount of clout I had built and, quite honestly, I was awfully proud of myself.

I'm So Confused

Cynthia Lambert

During the 1996-97 Stanley Cup season, Russian-born tennis sensation Anna Kournikova frequented Joe Louis Arena. Sometimes she watched practices while sitting with the family of Wings forward and fellow Russian Igor Larionov (I originally thought she was Igor's daughter). Other times I would see her waiting in the lower concourse outside the Wings' dressing room after games. Then came the rumors that Kournikova and Red Wings Russian phenom Sergei Fedorov were an item. The romantic cat-and-mouse game between the two was being played out amidst plenty of speculation in the media. It was a big deal. First, both were good looking and talented professional athletes. But the predominant reason for the all of the attention was that Kournikova was a mere 15 years old; Fedorov was 27. Were they an item or weren't they? If they were, Sergei was potentially breaking the law, considering the age of consent in Michigan was 16. Honestly, I didn't care if they were dating. But the sports world did, so I had to care.

Attention to the "non-relationship" piqued during the Wings Stanley Cup parade in June of 1997. There was Kournikova, now 16 years old, riding in the convertible car with Fedorov. Both waved to the fans in what seemed like a public acknowledgement of their relationship. Still, comments from Kournikova's camp and from the Wings were that the two were just good friends — two Russian-born super-athletes sharing the spotlight of success.

Regardless, this further ignited the chatter over whether or not they were a romantic item. Again, I didn't care. But one night, after a game during the 1997-98 season, I was forced to care, and on deadline. Kournikova approached me in the lower concourse as I made my way to the dressing room.

"Cyndy, look," she said, holding out her right hand to reveal a gold knotted ring threaded onto her ring finger.

"Nice," I said.

"But do you know what this means?" she asked. "It is from Sergei to me."

She was implying, of course, that she and Fedorov were married, or at minimum, engaged. I still wasn't buying it.

"But it's on the wrong hand, Anna," I countered, exposing my lack of knowledge regarding how things work in eastern European countries.

"Not in Russia," she explained. "In Russia you wear the ring on your right hand."

I took her word for it.

"So, are you two married?" I asked, needing to hear the words before I phoned The News *sports desk to save space on the front page.*

"What do you think?" she said, toying with me. "Sergei has one just like it."

At that point I needed to get in the dressing room to complete my reporting on the game ... and, yes, to check in with Fedorov on this twist of events. My job, already bordering on trivial compared to reporters who covered the crime beat, the environment, politics or even obituaries, took a further dive, dropping me to the status, albeit temporarily, of a society page reporter. After my cursory interviewing about the power play, goals scored and net-minding, I found Fedorov in the weight room. He would often retreat there to get away from the main part of the dressing room, which held the majority of the commotion and reporters.

"Hey Sergei, you got a minute?" I asked. He waved me into the room that was, generally speaking, off limits to reporters. I told him the story about Kournikova, the ring she wore and what she told me. Fedorov bristled.

"She bought that for herself!" he said, shaking his head. "To match mine. I don't want to talk about this anymore Cyndy."

End of story.

A gossip columnist or a society writer would certainly have followed up with more dogged questions to delve deeper, to make him break and declare the honest to God truth about his and Anna's entire relationship.

But … *I DIDN'T CARE!*

Though I did care about being played for a fool by Kournikova, sending me on her errand to prod Fedorov to divulge how he felt about her. The events of that night reminded me how silly teenage girls can be, even those who were gifted tennis players who made millions of dollars through the game, endorsements and modeling gigs.

As it turned out, a few years later it was rumored that Fedorov and Kournikova had indeed tied the knot. But this time it was Fedorov saying they were married and Kournikova denying it. Ah, young love. Or something like it.

13

Celebrity Encounters

Working at a job with daily access to professional athletes can diminish the WOW-factor when seeing or encountering "celebrities." Still, for me it took a couple of seasons before I lost the thrill factor when it came to star hockey players and former hockey greats. When I started in the business I was a sports fan first, and a writer/reporter second. I got into the field, not because of a love for writing, but a love of sports.

Outside of my early Marcel Dionne meet-and-greet thrill, I kept my excitement pretty well hidden. It helped that I began working with the likes of future notables Steve Yzerman, Sergei Fedorov, Adam Graves, Mike Modano and Eric Lindros when they were still teenagers or early in their careers. Because of this, their "star" status didn't affect me much. I cannot say the same was true with established hockey stars. Working with then-present-day legends such as Wayne Gretzky, Ray Bourque, Mario Lemieux, Patrick Roy, Mark Messier, Grant Fuhr and Mike Bossy left me tongue-tied and searching for my composure. Gladly, it took only a couple of years for that to fade, allowing me to do my job without getting all flushed in the face during one-on-one interviews.

But to the everyday fan, hockey players were stars. I was frequently reminded of this when stepping off the team bus at the hotel. Dozens of fans would be waiting for the team to arrive with a mission of getting an autograph, the chance to snap a picture or get a wave hello. It was satisfying to see how most of the players would stop to comply with the fans' requests.

But there were times when players were reluctant to sign autographs. Red Wings forward Shawn Burr was the most vocal about this issue, usually in hockey hotbeds such as Toronto or Chicago. Burr said he knew the "real" fans from those who just wanted autographs so they could sell them. He vowed he would give those in the latter category a piece of his mind and would absolutely NOT sign autographs for them.

Then Shawn would exit the bus and make his way to the hotel lobby door. Along the way, he would comply with every autograph seeker's request. Sometimes he would challenge the seekers of signatures, but in the end he would sign.

I never made a big deal about or had a strong opinion about the hockey fans swarming the team bus or with their requests for photos or autographs. That was the players' business, not mine. However, working as a hockey beat writer carried its own celebrity perks – movie stars who were hockey fans. Sometimes I was embarrassed by my own excitement at seeing an actor or actress up close. And the opportunities were frequent because many of Hollywood's stars were also sports fans. It was funny to witness a movie star smitten with the whole hockey experience.

Very early in my career, as I stood outside the dressing room at the Forum in Los Angeles, I (kind of) met my first celebrity. Because of the time zone difference, I had only a few minutes to grab some quotes from the players in both dressing rooms and the coaches before heading back to the press box to write my final story and freshen up my notebook for the last edition. Because of this, I was in a hurry and a bit stressed. This tight deadline was exacerbated if the team exceeded the rule for opening the dressing room door to the media after the game ended. The rule was 10 minutes after the final buzzer, but there were times when that rule was pushed beyond its limit.

On this night the hallway was lined with media members from the L.A. area and a small handful of us from Detroit. This was in my first year or two after taking over the hockey beat so I still didn't know many other members of the media. I turned to my right toward the closed dressing room door: no movement. I turned to my left and there, standing next to me, was a tall but plump man with curly hair. Though he stood 6'2" he seemed shorter because of his downcast eyes and head.

I did a double take, then blurted out: "Wow, hi!"

It was John Candy. Like many people I was a huge fan of his work and comedic style. And I had absolutely no idea what to say to him next. His response to my greeting was to shuffle his feet a bit as he looked down. Then he shyly said, "Hello."

"It's so nice to meet you," I said, bravely, though omitting my name.

The locker room doors then opened and, to keep from seeming like a stalker, I gave a nod and went back to my job. I never saw him again.

Another time in L.A., as I parked my rental car in the lot and made my way to the media entrance, I caught a glimpse of one of my favorite actresses: Goldie Hawn. She had just pulled up and was in the process of unloading her kids from the car, as she helped them get on their jackets and sweaters for the game. It struck me recently that her daughter and now accomplished actress Kate Hudson was probably among those I saw. Amidst Goldie doing this "normal" stuff, I do have to say that the most extraordinary thing I noticed about her was how absolutely tiny her waist was. I swear, it had to be 18 inches, if that. I am proud to say I resisted the urge to casually walk over to meet her. Instead, I hoofed it quickly to the press box and called my mom to tell her my news. She was a big Goldie fan, too.

Pretty much every game in Los Angeles had a subplot of I Spy. I always wanted to get there early to scout out the stands for celebrities. Many times other writers would point out someone who was in a TV show or movie. One of the most humorous of my scouting missions was when I caught sight of male model Fabio. It was midway through the first period when this guy with long flowing hair rose from his seat, shook his head so that his hair flowed around his shoulders, then strutted down the stairs and headed to the corridor. He must have run his hands through his hair five times in the 10 seconds it took to walk through the crowd. Then, as he turned I saw it was him. Not impressed.

The best encounters, though, were the ones that were completely unexpected. Like the time I was driving down Century Boulevard in Los Angeles one afternoon on my way to the Wings practice. I was stopped at a light. The weather was beautiful so I had the window rolled down.

"Excuse me, miss," came a very familiar voice in the car next to me, "Is this the way to the 405?"

Jay Leno, comedian and host of The Tonight Show, was sitting in a black Bentley and asking me for directions! Sure, he lived in L.A. and of course, he knew exactly where the 405 freeway was. I felt he knew initiating a quick conversation would give me a thrill. Or maybe he did that to give total strangers something fun to talk about. Or maybe he was hitting on me. I didn't care the reasoning. I was just charged up that I was talking to him.

"Yes!" I replied. "Yes it is!"

"Thank you," he said, with a smile.

My mouth opened and I had no idea what to say next. So I blurted out the most honest thing I could: "I love your comedy. You're so funny!"

"Thank you, thank you very much," he said, nodding, then waved and drove off.

Nothing was as unexpected as the time I stood in a line at the women's rest room in Vancouver at a Canucks game. At the time, the rest rooms used by the media were the same ones used by VIPs sitting in the most exclusive boxes.

As I waited in line, silently cursing the women taking their own sweet time, I looked at the woman in front of me. She was petite, but tall with hair more beautiful than Fabio's. As she turned – likely sensing me staring at her – I realized who it was: Farrah Fawcett. Much of my high school years were spent trying to get my hair to look like hers; and I came close during my senior year. I said hello to her, and she, in typical Farrah fashion, gave a huge smile and returned my greeting. We actually chatted for a few seconds about the long line and wondered out loud why the women wouldn't hurry. But the best part came when I told all my fellow reporters who I saw … and where I saw her. They went green with envy. Of course, they couldn't go to look for her where I had met her … because they were all men.

Up until that point, my celebrity encounters were all fleeting. Then came a Saturday afternoon in Buffalo. On this particular road trip, the Red Wings game against the Sabres was a Sunday matinee. By this time of day I had covered the practice and submitted my work to the paper. I was left with NOTHING to do.

Instead of spending the next eight hours reading a novel or watching television in my hotel room, I opted for the hotel workout room. As I let myself in I noticed two things. First, it was very small and, second, I was the only one there. I grabbed the TV remote control, tuned in to a scary movie and climbed on the only StairMaster in the room. I was also wearing very unattractive looking sweats and a worn out T-shirt. C'mon, it's the workout room in a Buffalo hotel on a Saturday afternoon. Who am I going to see?

I was about 10 minutes into my 30-minute workout when the door opened. In walked Miami Dolphins quarterback Dan Marino. If my hands had been on the heart rate monitor I would have reached new cardiovascular heights. What the heck was Dan Marino doing in a piddly little hotel workout room? He must have made a wrong turn, right?

He walked right over to me.

"Hi," he said. Hi?

"Hello," I said back, not daring to pursue a conversation because I know how weird I can get.

"Are you almost done on this machine?" he asked.

Without thinking, I blurted: "No."

To his credit, he didn't challenge me or use his well-established charm and stature to muscle me off the StairMaster. I respected that. Besides, looking at the two of us, I certainly needed the workout more than him.

"I've got another 20 minutes to go," I added.

I thought Dan would leave, but he didn't. After a few minutes of standing and watching my choice of Saturday afternoon television he asked if he could change the channel. I grudgingly gave up the remote. The last thing I wanted to watch was college football, and I knew that's where he was headed. Because I was around athletes and sports lingo seemingly all of the time, at times like this I just wanted to pretend sports didn't exist. I needed a break. But it would have been downright rude to tell one of the NFL's best quarterbacks that I not only wanted control of the StairMaster but the TV as well.

The next 20 minutes were excruciating. Not only was I aware that I couldn't exhibit poor form by hanging onto the handles of the machine (who doesn't?), but I thought I needed to preserve some dignity by not gasping for air when the workout got hard. When I finally wobbled off the machine after my 30-minute workout, my legs were shaking. It was then I understood for perhaps the first time just how good a workout the StairMaster could be when done properly. I gave a wave to Dan to officially turn over the machine to him and walked on my Jell-O legs to the elevator to spend the rest of the night watching my scary movies.

Even though all of these celebrity encounters were noteworthy for me, the one that will forever rank as No. 1 in my mind is the one that involved the "mystery man."

It was the late 1980s and Jacques Demers was the coach for the Wings. I, along with other media members, had been interviewing him after the game. I hung back to ask a follow-up question or two. As I listened to Jacques' answer I glanced outside of the office and saw a tall, good looking blond man standing with a dark haired gentleman. I had no idea who the latter was, but the former looked very familiar.

As I turned back to ask Jacques another question I heard one of the men outside say, "Wait, that's Cynthia Lambert. I want to meet her."

OK, this was getting weird … and frustrating. I was half-listening to Jacques because something inside told me that I should know who the blond was. OK, he's tall with an athletic build, I said to myself. Is he one of the Detroit Lions? Maybe one of the Detroit Tigers? No, that couldn't be. Why would he want to meet me? Is he a reporter? Maybe a national reporter? No. Again, how would he even know who I am?

Finally, my stream of questions for Jacques ran out as did his answers.

"Hey Shadow. Are you OK?" Jacques said to me, interrupting my train of thought. He called me the Shadow because he said I was always lurking behind him and he couldn't shake me. It was a term of endearment, I promise.

"Yeah, I'm good. Just organizing my notebook," I replied. Time had run out; I had to leave the office, still not knowing who the guy was. And he was waiting for me. As I stepped out of the office the tall blond man approached me.

"Hello Cynthia, I know you're very busy right now, but I just wanted to meet you," he said, extending his hand for me to shake. "I'm Jeff Daniels."

Had I been cool or even *thinking* I would have said something like, "Of course, Jeff, what a thrill to meet you. I'm a huge fan of your work. Thank you so much for introducing yourself to me."

Instead, I gave the universal, "duh," body language and touched my forehead with the palm of my hand, then blurted out, "That's who you are!"

There's no coming back from that one. Here is a big-time movie actor introducing himself to me and I didn't even try to hide the fact that I was struggling to pinpoint who he was. Everyone knew who he was. At that point in time Jeff had just come off his amazing performances in *Terms of Endearment* and *The Purple Rose of Cairo*, and seemed to be on the fast track in Hollywood. But because he lived in Chelsea, Michigan, about an hour drive from Detroit, he was also Red Wings fan – and apparently, someone who read my articles.

It was a huge compliment that he thought enough of me and my work to want to meet me. And I have never forgotten his humility and how excited he was to be in the Red Wings dressing room. What I thought most extraordinary was that he was free to roam into the main part of the dressing room, but, instead he stood in the hallway leading to the exit. It seemed as though he didn't want to disturb the routine in the dressing room or interfere with those who had work to do. I had such respect for him from that moment on. Because of this, and because of his talent, I have been a loyal fan of his through the years.

What makes my meeting Jeff so poignant to this day is that my son, Quinn, has attended several of the teen acting camps at Daniels' professional theater in Chelsea called the Purple Rose Theatre. In the Purple Rose, Daniels created a space for exceptional actors to practice their craft without having to leave their Midwestern roots for the marquees of New York City or lights of Hollywood. Quinn has yet to meet Jeff, but when he finally does, I'm sure it will be a great experience, just as it was for me.

Fedorov Gets the Assist

Cynthia Lambert

Despite the ongoing opportunity, I collected very few hockey artifacts during my career. I guess I figured I would be surrounded by the posters, pictures, trinkets and other notable items for the rest of my life. Why collect them? Above all, my general rule was that I didn't ask for autographs. I had only broken this rule once, asking Wayne Gretzky, Brett Hull, Joe Kocur and Bob Probert to sign photos to give to my nephews one Christmas. (They were a big hit — especially with my brothers.)

But a situation at my house prompted me to completely break this rule and shamelessly ask for autographs. In 1995 I had just bought my first house and wanted a deck built off a back door. I said this at a gathering that included my brother Steve's sister-in-law, Julie. Her husband, Paul Fayad, heard my wish and jumped on it. Paul owns a number of businesses but actually enjoys doing home improvements and building things in his spare time. He was also a huge hockey fan. Within days he had the lumber ordered and arranged for his buddies to help him with the heavy lifting. It was early fall and if the deck was completed quickly I still had time to enjoy it that year.

After weeks of coming over to my house after work, Paul was near to finishing the deck that was adorned with decorative railings and stairs to enter the backyard. It was beautiful and everything I had hoped for. During the whole building process Paul asked only one thing of me. He wanted to know the "scoop" about the Wings.

"Tell me something you know but you're not writing," he ordered.

Paul wouldn't accept money as payment for his time, but I knew I had to compensate him somehow. Then I came up with a brilliant idea.

I drove to Eastside Sports, which, at the time, supplied the Wings with their uniforms. I met with the owner and told him my mission. Paul was a huge fan of the Russian Five — Viacheslav Fetisov, Igor Larionov, Vladimir Konstantinov, Sergei Fedorov and Vyacheslav Kozlov — so I thought getting him a Fetisov jersey would be the way to go. I ended up buying two of Fetisov's actual game jerseys – one for Paul and one for myself. I thought the world of the man I called Slava-bear. Then I got an idea that would be the icing on the cake – get them autographed by the Russian Five. This is where the shameless part comes in.

I brought both of the jerseys to the next practice at Joe Louis Arena, concealed in a paper bag along with a Sharpie pen. After conducting my interviews, I began my autograph request with Sergei. Sergei, though very nice, could sometimes be a bit persnickety.

"Sergei, I know this is really unprofessional, but someone did something really nice for me and I wanted to get the five of you to sign this Fetisov jersey," I explained. "And I thought I would get one for myself, too. Is there any way you would sign this for me?"

Fedorov looked at me and without pausing, motioned for me to hand him the bag. He signed both jerseys then winked at me.

"I'll take care of this, Cyndy," he said, getting up, still in his skates, and walking over toward Igor.

"No Sergei!" I nearly shouted. "I'll take them around; I just wanted you to sign them."

"Cyndy, let me do this," he said, handing the jerseys to Larionov, pointing toward me and saying something to him in Russian. Larionov signed them, then handed them Fetisov, who sat next to him. Fetisov looked at the back of the jersey, saw his name and the No. 2 on the back and smiled at me. Then he signed them both. Fedorov again collected the two jerseys and headed to Konstantinov. After playfully shouting at me about not getting his jerseys and vowing he wouldn't sign them, he grabbed the Sharpie pen from Sergei and signed both. Then came Kozlov, who was treated like the baby brother by the other four Russian players. At first, Kozlov scoffed, indicating he didn't have time to sign. Sergei had none of this and pushed the jerseys nearly into Kozlov's face and ordered him to sign them ... which he did.

Within a couple of minutes Sergei accomplished what I knew would have taken me close to an hour to do, likely uttering apologies *and worrying about being "found out" all along the way. The jerseys signed, Sergei stuffed them back into paper bag and handed them back to me with a smile. "There you go!" he said.*

When I delivered the autographed jersey to Paul, he couldn't speak. To this day he counts it as one of his most prized possessions, but one he would eventually like to present to Fetisov. It was, indeed, the perfect gift. And it was the perfect gift to myself, too.

14

Taking Advantage of Access

Friends and family members also benefited from my job when they were able to experience some of the behind-the-scenes activity and VIP access. The key, I learned, was to not abuse the perk. This would have been easy to do, considering the generous nature of those involved in the sport of hockey ... especially the athletes. It was a rare week when a fan or friend of a player or media member wasn't in the dressing room after a practice or game. Sometimes it was the result of a winning bid at a high-priced charity auction; other times it was just ... because.

Of course, helping to keep me in line were the ethics of being a professional reporter. I could not accept any sort of gratuity or gift from any person or organization I covered, as it could potentially sway my coverage of that team, player, coach, etc. While this was usually easy to stick to, there were some tempting times – giveaways that I could not accept because of who was offering them, meals that I could not eat because of who was paying for them and so on. That said, there were times when the "source" would send items directly to my home – NHL commemorative coins from the league, publications said to be collectors' issues, posters, and other items

I ended up keeping because, honestly, I didn't have the time or inclination to mail them back. There were also the NHL All-Star Game and Stanley Cup Finals swag bags given to the media. These collections of gifts contained some really cool items – jackets, travel bags, pens, leather-bound notebooks, coffee mugs. I accepted those, then parceled off most of the items to friends or family members, keeping very few as remembrances. One I do still have is a blue jean shirt with the logo from the 1994 Stanley Cup finals between the New York Rangers and Vancouver Canucks.

The best score ever came during an All-Star Game when I – along with most other NHL media members – accepted the invitation to a party hosted by NHL sponsor Nike. Nike was new to the sport of ice hockey and had the Wings' Sergei Fedorov on the line to wear their interesting, if not odd, white skates to lead their marketing efforts. I didn't technically "cover" Nike, so I felt no significant conflict of interest. Upon arriving at the swanky event, each attendee was given a gift bag containing some low-priced goodies: pens, notebooks, stuff like that. We were then asked to fill out a short form, checking the box for our preference: Nike hockey skates or Nike inline skates. This certainly was a big-time score and one that I doubted would actually come to fruition. My fellow media members and I made a pact to let each other know if and when our "package" arrived at our doorstep. We all pretty much believed that we would receive a coupon in the mail to purchase the skates, perhaps with a substantial discount, but not the actual skates. So I filled out the form, opting for what I believed to be the less expensive inline skates.

About a month later, a packaged arrived at my doorstep – white and lime green Nike inline skates. I guess they weren't lying. And they were pretty cool. But there was no brake on them, meaning they were for serious inline hockey players. That was certainly not me. As I did with many of my hockey paraphernalia items, I walked the skates down to a neighbor's house. They had three young girls. I would often see the oldest girl, Sara VanRaemdonck, skating up and down the street in her inline skates. She was, to be sure, serious about roller hockey. In fact, many days the street would be clogged with about a dozen kids from the neighborhood playing hockey – most of them girls – wearing Red Wings jerseys, T-shirts or sweatshirts. I delivered the skates to the "Van's" house, telling the kids' ecstatic mom, Sally, that I hoped the skates fit. They did. Sarah skated in them for years, wearing out the wheels and ordering more from Nike. She ended up being a star roller hockey player for Grosse Pointe North High School and was forever grateful for the sweet skates I gave her. I chalked that up to an excellent use of swag!

Growing up in a sports-focused family, it would have been easy for my brothers, cousins or others to besiege me with requests to meet the players or get them free tickets to the games, although I never got free tickets until after I retired from the job. But my family and friends never asked for anything. They were content to get the inside scoop on the players at family gatherings, or simply to have a hockey insider available to bounce off their theories and opinions.

Because of this, it was always gratifying to invite family members or close friends to participate in some sort of hockey affair. My brother Steve remembers the time I invited him to bring his son to a practice. I had cleared it with the team beforehand and Steve was thrilled to see the Wings in action. My nephew, Bret, was about 18 months old at the time – a toddling teething machine who couldn't care less about hockey, much less pronounce the word. I told a few of the players that the man and child in the stands were my brother and nephew. Throughout the practice, the players would wave to Steve, make faces at Bret and then shout to Steve how his sister was a lousy reporter. It was a good time for all.

When practice ended, Steve Yzerman called my brother and Bret over to the tunnel area that led to the dressing room. Yzerman took the stick he had been using during the practice and gave it to Bret. My brother Steve was near speechless but managed to carry on a bit of a conversation with the Wings team captain. After Yzerman walked away my brother looked down at his son. Bret was gnawing on the stick – a brand new wooden teething toy.

One of the most memorable games I covered took place at the old Chicago Stadium and involved a few friends of mine. They decided to make the trip to Chicago for the weekend game, so I took a day or two off after the game so we could enjoy the windy city. I rarely took any time off during the season, so I was ready to cut loose.

The Red Wings always stayed at the Drake Hotel in Chicago, which meant I did too. Without fail, I would get my room key, take the elevator to my floor and open the door to reveal an expansive room with two large beds and couch that converted into a sleeper sofa. It was the perfect lodging for me and my three friends.

They were waiting for me in the lobby as I arrived at the hotel. I went to the front desk to check in and get my room key. As we rode up in the elevator I described how beautiful the rooms were, how it was going to be a great stay for all of us, how pampered we were going to feel. We arrived at the room, I opened the door and walked into the smallest hotel room I'd ever seen. There was one twin bed pushed up against a wall, a diminutive desk with a phone on it and a miniscule bathroom with small shower – no tub. After my friend Paula busted out laughing, I headed down to the front desk to see if they would switch my room, which, thankfully, they did. Moments later we were in not just a large hotel room, but one of the luxurious suites at the historic hotel.

The game was the next afternoon. I had made arrangements for my friends to purchase tickets through the Blackhawks, which meant they were getting seats usually available to the players. Before I get into what happened at the game, I need to paint the picture. None of my friends were sports fans. Paula loved auto racing and had an appreciation for athleticism. My other friends, Kelly and Sue, not so much. Kelly was also a wild card in this situation. A police officer at the time, Kelly assumed she would be bored with the game. Her plan was to walk around "looking at the gift shops." Of course, there were no "shops" at Chicago Stadium, just beer, hot dogs and more beer. I gave instructions to Paula to keep a low profile and make sure

Kelly and Sue did as well. I explained that the Chicago fans were not tolerant of visiting fans and I wanted my three friends to leave the game in one piece.

The groundwork laid, we hopped into a cab and went to the stadium. Their seats were amazing, in the lower bowl, close to the ice. They were close enough to smell the ice and hear the players. After leaving them at their seats, I gave another word of warning.

"I'm serious Kelly, behave!"

"Cyndy, just go do your job and leave us alone," Kelly snapped … or something on that order.

During the first intermission I met them in the concourse. Paula looked in a state of panic. Kelly's face was bright red, her eyes wild. Sue couldn't stop laughing.

"This is so exciting!" Kelly said. "The players are so fast!"

I had never seen Kelly this excited over anything, let alone a sport. She was most certainly bit by the hockey bug. But her excitement left Paula worried for their safety.

"She is not behaving," Paula said between gritted teeth. "At one point, one of the Blackhawks tripped one of the Red Wings and Kelly stood up and screamed, 'You Blackhawks are nothing but a bunch of sissy-trippers!' There are all these guys in front of us. They turned around and mouthed, 'Sissy-trippers?' She's going to get us killed!"

Kelly vowed to tone it down, a promise she went back on minutes into the second period. As the game progressed, the most rabid of the Blackhawks fans in their section became more impassioned and more drunk. It was a close game too, with the Wings holding onto a two-goal lead. When the Blackhawks scored to pull within one goal, the largest of the tough-talking Hawks' fans turned and yelled at Kelly.

"In your face!" he bellowed.

Not missing a beat, Kelly, in a sing-song voice usually reserved for little girls jumping rope, replied to him: "But we're still ahead of you-u!"

Her response was so bizarre that the Blackhawks fan had no idea how to reply. Oddly, as a result, the situation died down.

After the Wings won the game and I finished writing my articles, my friends met me in the concourse so that we could head back to the Drake to get ready for a night on the town. Paula and Sue definitely need a glass of wine to decompress from the experience. But Kelly was still flying high from her first exposure to professional hockey.

The Best and the Worst

Cynthia Lambert

I'm not a big believer in casting dispersions toward anyone, particularly those who have reached the pinnacle of their dream career – coaching in the NHL. But sometimes the people who achieve these heights use their power to bully others.

I worked hard to get along with and respect NHL coaching legend Scotty Bowman for who he was – an eccentric, brilliant and successful hockey coach. But at the same time, he could be a challenging person to work with day in and day out. He had his old-school ways that I respected, but some odd methods that I never understood. One of Scotty's strategies was to keep people guessing, whether it was not offering a player information about where he stood in the pecking order of the lineup or playing coy with reporters about who was going to start in net. More than once I thought I had figured out Scotty – when he was merely hinting and when he was actually giving me a scoop. He got me good one night when we shared an elevator ride down to the lobby of the hotel before a game. Bowman looked at me and said, "Vernon."

He was indicating that, though he would usually never tell the media who was going to be in goal that night, he was letting me in on the scoop. He was telling me that Mike Vernon would get the start. This was newsworthy because Chris Osgood was the more obvious choice at that point and for that opponent.

"Really?" I replied, still not sure if Scotty was being honest or toying with me.

"Yeah, I'm going with Vernon. Just wanted you to know."

When I arrived at the arena, I phoned the copy desk at the paper and told them to add that Vernon "was expected to get the start." The phrase "was expected" was my savior, because a couple of hours later, Chris Osgood led the team onto the ice for the game, an indication that he was getting the start. Bowman 1; Lambert 0.

155

I'd like to think that Scotty made me a better reporter but working with him on a daily basis sure was frustrating at times. Fortunately, he was the only coach I ever had any issues with. To my amazement, even the most seasoned, gnarly and legendary coaches were perfectly pleasant to deal with. I think the one who surprised me the most was Toronto Maple Leafs coach John Brophy. He carried with him a reputation of old time hockey rawness and a wicked tongue. Yet, he was always kind and helpful to me, which completely altered his longstanding reputation ... at least in my eyes.

Generally speaking, coaches treated me without any prejudice. And some, such as the St. Louis Blues' Brian Sutter, compromised who he was, in a sense, to treat me with even more respect than he afforded the male reporters. Sutter came from a family rich in NHL success. In a remarkable multiple feat, one that has never been replicated in any sport that I am aware of, Sutter and his five brothers all made it to the NHL as players. Brian then went on to coach the Blues, among other teams in his rather lengthy coaching career. A hard-nosed player, Sutter was equally passionate as a coach. And that passion transferred into his way of expressing his anger or frustration after particularly hard losses. In other words, the expletives flew out of Sutter's mouth like they were part of an operatic aria. Though, and I'm guessing, because of his upbringing, Sutter did his best not to swear in front of me.

One night, after his St. Louis Blues were thrashed by the Wings, Sutter's emotions were simmering, and underneath that was a powder keg.

"I'm so sick and tired of these ... these ... guys and their ... their ... BAD ... work ethic," Sutter spat out, the curses being swallowed before being given life. This went on for a few sentences before he simply couldn't do it anymore.

"I'm really sorry Cynthia, but I need to say this. ... These fucking guys ... my apologies Cynthia ... and their fucking shitty work ethic ... sorry Cynthia ... I'm just so goddam sick of their fucking

*laziness ... Cynthia, I'm sorry ..." His tirade went on like this for
some time, bouncing from profanity to apologies to me – not to any of
the other dozen or so reporters standing there, just me. I have always
felt that was one of the kindest things any coach did for me, trying to
control his language to protect my "sensitive" ears.*

15

The Ever-expanding Job

After a number of years on the beat, giving me ample time to prove myself, I started to get approached by other media outlets to work for them as a contributor. For many beat writers, this was the gravy, the little perks that made all the hours of chasing down rumors, the endless months of travel, the short nights and long days all worthwhile.

Although I had confidence in my reporting skills it always shocked me when a news outlet wanted to pay me to tell them what I knew – and was already reporting in *The Detroit News*. From the newspaper's perspective, this was effective marketing of their product and of their resource (me). I also think that hearing about sports from a woman, even in the mid-1990s, was still a bit of a novelty.

So when Detroit radio legend J.P. McCarthy called, asking if I could be his hockey insider, the answer was a firm, "yes" from me. I gladly inherited this freelance gig from previous Red Wings/NHL beat writer Vartan Kupelian, who was considered to be one of the best in the business. Because of this, I felt pressure to measure up and not cause J.P. – host of the area's top-rated morning program on AM or FM radio – to look elsewhere. I also knew they were taking a leap of faith with me, someone who was, as of yet, unproven.

What I quickly learned working with J.P. once a week was that I had only 30-60 seconds to share the most important or interesting facets of a game played the night before, the analysis of an upcoming game or the scoop of a situation brewing with the team or players. Considering it always took me a while to get to the point when writing or talking, this was a real challenge for me. As a side note: I would bury the lead in most articles I wrote. This means backing into the real story by first writing a sentence or paragraph that was unnecessary. I even did this in game stories. I solved this problem by lopping off the first paragraph of everything I wrote. It was a self-editing technique that worked like magic. *(And yes, one of my editors encouraged me to delete the first chapter of this book, which I did. Old habits die hard I suppose.)*

I loved being on the radio. It ignited an adrenaline response I could feed off and use. It was why I originally wanted to pursue a career in journalism. But J.P.'s show was an early morning program, meaning his producer would call me before 7 a.m., sometimes sooner. Considering the earliest I would ever make it back home after a game at Joe Louis Arena was about midnight, my radio gig often made for short nights. Even worse was when the Wings played on the West Coast. My hotel phone would ring around 3 or 3:30 in the morning. The producer would tell me what J.P. wanted to discuss, then put me on hold for about 10 seconds before J.P. opened the line. During those 10 seconds I would sit up in bed and start doing my own version of a vocal warmup. I would raise my voice high, speak softly, loudly, anything to shake the sleep out of my tone. When J.P. clicked over to open up the phone line he and I would chat for a minute or so. It was always a friendly conversation, but it was fast. No dead air, to be sure. He would thank me for my time; I would hang up and go right back to sleep.

Sportscaster Dave LewAllen then asked me in the mid-1990s if I would periodically come on the *Sunday Sports Update* program that aired late on Sunday evening on Detroit's ABC affiliate, WXYZ. This opened up a whole new world and one that I was not necessarily completely comfortable with. There was no hiding how I looked and no way to erase the first few sentences I spoke. My radio gig with J.P. helped teach me how to be more precise with the spoken word, but TV was so … visual. This required a bit more effort on my part, including fixing my hair, putting on makeup, wearing something nice and driving to the studio, a good half hour away. Once I got there, I enjoyed the experience of talking shop with Dave. The key was for me to forget about the camera and just focus on the conversation. Dave was a polite and smart interviewer so these TV appearances usually came off well and I was on my way back home shortly after our bit was recorded.

Though the broadcast freelancing was both good money and exposure, there were two print opportunities that I enjoyed the most, mainly because of the prestige factor. Fairly early in my career I was asked by Bob McKenzie, editor of *The Hockey News* – better known as the hockey bible – if I would be the Red Wings contributor to the publication. Not only was *The Hockey News* pretty much the official record of all things NHL and read throughout North America, but it was also published and available around the world. I gladly and proudly accepted this job and wrote for *The Hockey News* until I stepped down from the beat in 1998. Every so often I would be asked by someone at *The Hockey News* to write a feature article about the Wings organization or a player. This became a more frequent request as the team got better and as they headed to their back-to-back Stanley Cups in 1997 and 1998. Although there were times when the last thing I wanted to do was crank out another article in a week's time, I never came close to begging off the job, always remembering what an achievement it was to write for the weekly hockey bible.

As the Wings continued to move up in the standings and make bigger and better showings in the NHL playoffs, my knowledge was even more in demand. Other local radio stations asked me to appear on their shows, reporters from other NHL cities called to get the goods on the Wings and national publications were beginning to take more notice of the Red Wings. It was then that I got the call from *Sports Illustrated* asking if I could be the official stringer, or contact person, for the Red Wings. Before I knew what it entailed,

I said yes. I would be a fool not to. Then I got the details, which were mind-blowingly simplistic. Someone from the *SI* team would contact me to get background information that would then be compiled and provided to a reporter/writer at the magazine who would use the information as starter-fodder. The reporter/writer would then follow up with his or her sources, coaches, players, etc. to create the article. In other words, I was the first touchpoint in Detroit for hockey. Every time I spoke with the contact at *SI* they would pay me. Sometimes when one of their reporters sat with me at a game to get background information for a larger, more esoteric piece, I would get a check. Easier money was never made.

While those money-making endeavors were very satisfying, it was the casual conversations or phone calls I took at home from certain people in the NHL that gave me the biggest kick. One of my favorites was Canadian Broadcasting Company (CBC) commentator and former NHL coach Don Cherry. There were some who said Cherry was sexist, and, although at one time he spoke out about women going in the dressing room, he never challenged me on my position nor was he ever anything but pleasant, respectful and hilarious. I'd like to think Don and I became friends through the years – we exchanged Christmas cards and could talk for a half hour or more about his favorite player, Bob "Probie" Probert: his on-ice prowess and, sadly, any current legal issues Probert was having. Nothing ignited Don Cherry more than hockey fights … especially those that involved Probert winning handily or the Colorado Avalanche's Claude Lemieux being pummeled.

While Cherry has established himself as a loud, opinionated and passionate hockey expert, when we talked he was always soft-spoken and a gentleman, especially when he would talk about his wife, Rose, his home or his dogs, Blue and then Blue II. For me, to be accepted and befriended by Don Cherry, gave me a sense of overall acceptance into the NHL fraternity. Something that I had been striving for since my first day in the press box.

The Most Inappropriate Question

Cynthia Lambert

Reporters are paid to be inquisitive and curious. But sometimes that job requirement morphs into pure, unadulterated nosiness. I was not immune to that negative part of the job, but I did my best to keep my questioning on the up-and-up and not fall into the tabloid realm. But there was one time I couldn't help myself.

Russian-born player Sergei Fedorov, described by NHL greats Wayne Gretzky and Steve Yzerman – among others – as one of the best to ever play the game, was at times both secretive and open. I loved this dichotomy that was Sergei, and he has always held a special place in my heart. I think he was trusting, but felt he needed to be guarded because of his meteoric rise to fame and, in 1994, fortune.

In his first four NHL seasons, Sergei's annual salary was just a smidge above $250,000. This was before NHL players began demanding compensation more in line with other major professional athletes. In the 1993-94 season, Fedorov earned $295,000. His contract for the next season – after the huge change in NHL players' salary demands – was negotiated at nearly $3 million. Though he ended up making substantially less than that (about $1.7 million) due to the lockout by NHL owners, he had officially entered the megabucks world of earnings.

Shortly after Sergei signed that multi-million dollar contract, the Wings were in Chicago for a game. He was working on his stick outside the visitor's locker room – using a blowtorch to create the exact bend he wanted in the blade. We were talking about nonsensical things, topics that had little to do with the approaching game, his stats or the Wings power play. During a lull in the conversation, my nosey nature kicked in.

"Sergei, can I ask you a very personal question, not for publication?" I posed.

"Yeah; I guess," he replied.

"What's it like to make that kind of money?" I always wanted to ask that question but never felt comfortable posing it to any of the growing number of NHL millionaires.

Sergei thought for a moment, not offended in the least by my question. After a moment, he replied. "It's unbelievable," he said, then paused. "It's unbelievable what they take out in taxes."

With that, he bid adieu and went back into the locker room, only to emerge just as I was about to walk away.

"Cyndy, I want you to know that I don't think I deserve this amount of money," he said. "But I lived a long time without any. My parents had no money. I'm sending a lot of it back home, for them and my brother."

How many professional athletes would actually admit that they knew they didn't deserve to make more in a week than most people make in a year? This peek into who Sergei was made the news about him that much more disheartening in the years that followed. The financial advisor Sergei hired later in his career, and trusted completely, had absconded with tens of millions of dollars belonging to Sergei.

16

Unforgettable Kindness

Considering the unrelenting schedule of games and practices, along with time spent following trade rumors and other news, sports beat writers often spend more time with the athletes, coaches and team administrators they cover than with their own family members or friends. If the locker room is a hostile or contentious environment, a reporter's work life can be a living hell. I was lucky because my daily trip into the Red Wings' or visiting team's locker room lacked drama. In fact, much of the time it was a fun place to be. I was privy to some of the inside jokes and comments made between players, not to mention the luxury of having a consistent diet of drilled-down assessments of what transpired during a game from the players' perspectives. I also made it a practice to chat with the players and coaching staff about non-hockey stuff – movies, books, TV shows, music, current events. This helped me to get to know them a bit better in a nonthreatening way. Plus it made the job more enjoyable.

Because of this approach I developed professional friendships with many of the players, coaches, managers and owners. I was always aware, however, that a line of professionalism existed and I was cautious not to cross it. That said, there were times when I dipped my toe across that line for a singular autograph or odd question. One of these times began when I accepted an autograph from my mom's favorite player.

Sadly, this "favorite" player ended up leaving Detroit under some less-than-favorable circumstances, making him a preferred visiting villain to heckle upon his return to the Joe Louis Arena ice with his current team. Also, during his time wearing the winged wheel, he never quite consistently met or exceeded the expectations many in the Red Wings front office set for him. The player was Keith Primeau ... big No. 55.

Detroit drafted Keith third overall in the NHL's 1990 entry draft. He was a junior hockey phenom who was both skilled and tough. The Wings saw in him a player who was talented enough to score 30 goals a season and big enough – he was 6'5" and 220 pounds – to keep opponents honest. For some reason, the two of us clicked right from the beginning. He talked to me like I was his older sister; and I treated him like a little brother. I remember his first training camp. Keith sat in the stands, furious that he was asked to play left wing, instead of his natural position of center.

"Why the hell did they draft me if they don't want me to play center?" the 18-year-old Primeau scoffed.

Ah yes, youth. He had gone from being the big-time star in junior hockey to a situation where he was just one of many talented skaters on the ice at the NHL training camp – skaters who included centers Steve Yzerman and Sergei Fedorov, recently delivered from Russia where he had already earned star status. Unless Keith wanted to play third-line, he was going to have to adjust and move from his position as a center ... that was, if he was going to make the team at all. It was the proverbial rude awakening for a guy who had been a celebrated player to watch for a decade. Despite his frustration and anger about his current situation, he, fortunately, still had a sense of humility.

"Would you get off it," I told him bluntly one day. "You're an 18-year-old kid at an NHL training camp. This is when you listen and do what they tell you to do." Yes, I was rooting for him.

"This just pisses me off!" he countered.

Likely after many talks with his father and the Wings coaching staff, and a whole lot of hard work, Keith came around and had an impressive 14+ years in the NHL before a concussion knocked him out of the game for good.

While Keith's career progressed with the Red Wings, my hockey-crazed mom, Lois, adopted him as her new favorite Red Wing. She used to refer to him as "her little sweetie." There were even times when she would get upset with me for being too critical of him on the midseason report card.

"Really, Mom?" I would ask. "I'm the one you need to stand by, not him!" She would laugh, but give me a pinch to let me know she meant it.

In January of 1992 my mother was diagnosed with advanced-stage lung cancer. Despite going to the doctor repeatedly months before to seek a diagnosis that would explain why she felt so poorly, her doctor only ordered an X-ray, which showed nothing. Finally, after about eight months of her health inexplicably going downhill – and her primary care physician suggesting she see a psychiatrist to address her phantom symptoms – my mother's lung collapsed due to the size of the tumor. She needed immediate surgery to remove the lung and to capture and remove any other visible cancer in the area. Her brilliant thoracic surgeon, Dr. Luis Camero, did his best to get all of it, but there was one spot he couldn't extract. He provided a cautionary prognosis that the surgery went very well, but he was concerned about that one spot he could not remove. Chemo, radiation and experimental therapies awaited my mother, who was only 56 years old.

This had a devastating impact on me. My mom and I were best friends. We would talk at around 8:30 a.m. every day to touch base. I would share any news or, better yet, fun stories that happened. She would apprise me of what was going on in her life and tell me a funny story or two.

I told my mom everything about my job. She knew what information players had told me off the record, who was genuinely nice and who was a bit of a jerk. She asked questions about how I knew about trades, what different players and coaches were like and if I thought the Wings were going to sweep the next road trip. I think in many ways my mother lived vicariously through me. Before she met my dad she worked as a reservation agent for Republic Airlines and then United Airlines. She wanted to travel and experience independence. But when she met my dad, she knew she was destined for marriage and a family. Though she returned to United Airlines briefly when my brothers and I ranged in ages from 8 to 12, it was a pace she couldn't maintain and still be the kind of mom she wanted to be. So she quit and stayed home to selflessly support the rest of us in our endeavors and dreams.

Every road trip I went on, I would call from the hotel to check in with her and describe what the room looked like, what type of toiletries were in the bathroom and what the view was out my window. Traveling with a pro sports team, the hotels were usually top of the line so the amenities and locations were usually well worth talking about. And when my travel days were lengthened due to cancelled or delayed flights, she was always there with a perky comment or funny story about what was going on back in the Detroit area to keep me going.

So when my mother was in critical condition, I was a wreck. I took some days off work to be there for her and my dad, and to try my best to comprehend the gravity of what was happening to her and our family. When I went back to work, the team had been informed. Hockey is like that. One person hears news like this and word spreads … in a benevolent way. Several of the players and the coaches asked me how my mom was doing. My mom loved hearing which players asked about her, somehow feeling connected to them, as if they knew her personally.

When Keith approached me and asked about her, I shared that he was her favorite player, adding that she would be beyond thrilled that he asked about her.

"What's your mom's name?" he asked.

"Lois," I told him.

"OK," he replied. And that was it.

A few days later I was out of town, covering the Wings on

their road trip. I don't recall where we were – I was traveling in an emotional fog. I thought the time away would do me some good; to disconnect from the sadness at home and reconnect with my passion of reporting. After the Wings' practice, I hitched a ride on the team bus back to the hotel. As I was stepping off the bus, Keith yelled for me to hold up. He discretely handed me something. It was his hockey card, signed: "To Lois, I wish you all the best, Keith."

"Do you think your mom would want that?" he asked. "You don't have to take it."

I was so touched that he would initiate this act of kindness for someone he had never met. And I could already picture how my mom would react when I gave it to her.

"She's going to love it. Thank you so much," I said, and placed the card in my wallet so it wouldn't get bent or blemished.

When I returned home I drove to my parents' house and presented my mom with the gift from Keith. She clasped it in her hands, held it to her heart and broke into a huge smile ... something we didn't see often at that point.

For months my mom underwent therapies to stop the progression of the one spot that couldn't be removed during the initial surgery. In May of 1992 she finished chemo and we were hopeful that she had dodged the bullet. But at the following appointment to discuss her most recent CT scan, we were given the bad news. It was back.

Things spiraled downward pretty fast from there. My mom's positive and hopeful attitude struggled to regain its footing and the rest of us were once again sent scrambling to arrange our thoughts and reign in our emotions so that we could continue going to work and living our lives despite the dire situation she faced. My brothers and I all worked. My dad, a retired Detroit police officer, worked security detail at Detroit Riverview Hospital. All of their jobs kept them within a half hour of my mom. Mine could potentially take me as far away as Vancouver, easily a half-day trip from Detroit. I remember feeling so conflicted about road trips. They would pull me away from my mom, who needed me. But they would also add normalcy to my life; they could keep me grounded and sane, and recharge my emotional battery. So I continued to work, a decision she supported wholeheartedly.

By October of that year, we could see where my mom's road pointed. She tried every possible treatment and therapy, but to no avail. Dr. Camero seemed to always be there for her, offering encouragement or, when that could not be mustered, a sympathetic ear.

It was at this point that Keith approached me in the locker room after a practice. We were standing in the middle of the room with players, reporters and TV crews milling about.

"Hey Cynd, how's your mom doing?" he asked, innocently.

I'm not quite sure why I broke at that point, but I did. No words could come out of my mouth and tears began to well in my eyes.

Keith had the look of panic in his eyes.

"Oh shit, don't do that! Everyone's gonna think I'm making you cry," he said.

He led me to the short walkway connecting the main locker room to the weight room. Then he asked again. And I told him.

"Not good," I choked. "Not good at all."

It was all I could say. There was nothing more to it.

"Tomorrow," he said. "Tomorrow after practice I'm going to follow you to your parents' house so I can visit her. Do you think that would be OK?"

I was stunned at his suggestion. I also had no idea if it was OK or not. My mom had very little energy, spending much of the day lying on the couch. But she did shower and dress every day, regardless of how she felt. My mom had amazing strength and optimism. She wanted so desperately to live.

I called my dad after the practice to tell him of Keith's offer. My dad was not one to get too excited about anything. He lived his 79-year life with a blood pressure that never got over 100/60. He was a methodical golfer (a scratch handicap at one point), a former Marine who served in Korea and a cop who navigated through the 1967 riots in Detroit without bringing home any of the ugliness he saw. He was truly a gentle man. But when he got really, really excited, he would say something like: "Oh." or "That would be nice."

When I told him of the offer, he paused. At first I thought it was to think about whether he wanted to accept. But when he spoke, I could tell he had first needed to collect himself. Then he gave approval by saying: "Well, that would be very nice!"

The next day, Keith followed me to my parents' home in St. Clair Shores – a quick 20 minute drive from downtown. We entered through the side door. I could see my mom laying on the couch. I motioned for Keith to wait and I walked into the living room.

"There's my daughter!" my mom said, sitting up slowly. She was wearing one of her Red Wings sweatshirts (no doubt, the work of my dad, who was also wearing one). "What a nice surprise."

After hugging her I told her that someone else was here to see her. Keith walked into the living room and my mom sprang up off the couch like she had just gotten an electrical jolt. She hadn't moved that fast in months.

Keith walked over to my mom, helped her up and gave her a bear hug. He then made himself at home, plopping down in a chair across from the couch and began to talk. He asked her questions, talked to my dad, shared a few hockey stories, told them what a horrible reporter I was, and so on. He stayed for about 45 minutes before heading home to his family.

For about a half hour after Keith left, my mom enjoyed the remnants of her adrenalin buzz. She thanked me profusely for arranging it. But I couldn't take credit. I had just led Keith to her house so he could share his kindness and compassion.

My mother passed away a few weeks later. I was at my parent's house to help my dad sort through some of my mom's things, including her purse. As I reached into a zipped area of her handbag, I found the autographed Keith Primeau card, safely enclosed in a plastic cover. She took it with her everywhere ... a favorite gift from her favorite player.

Gone Too Soon

Cynthia Lambert

In any profession – and in life, in general – there are people who touch our lives. Sometimes we become fast friends, other times we can observe them from a distance and learn from their strength and struggles.

During my days covering the Red Wings I was privileged to connect with many special men who happen to excel at the sport of ice hockey. Four of them had their lives end all too soon. But in the short time I knew them, I felt a connection. They all brought special gifts to this world and left behind much sadness when they passed on.

Steve Chiasson was drafted by the Red Wings in 1985, a promising young defenseman who reached his potential playing for the Wings through the 1993-94 season before moving on to play for Calgary and then the Hartford Whalers, which became the Carolina Hurricanes. But Chiasson, like many people in our society, struggled with alcohol addiction. I'm not sure of the details of his battle, whether he tried to quit, went through rehab, joined AA or simply tried to manage his addiction on his own. What I do know was that he was a kind and honest man who worked hard at his craft and loved his family.

In 1999, when he was playing for the Hurricanes, Chiasson made a bad decision. Actually, it was a series of bad decisions, culminating in the horrific and instantaneous loss of his life.

That night, after losing to the Boston Bruins in the playoffs, the Hurricanes flew back to North Carolina and assembled for an end-of-season gathering at player Gary Roberts' house. Chiasson had been in the garage with teammates Ron Francis and Keith Primeau, drinking and talking. Francis told the two he was going into the house to call cabs to take all of the players home. Chiasson and Primeau also left the garage for the house to wait for the cabs. It was then that Chiasson made his fatal decision. Unbeknownst to his teammates, instead of waiting for the caravan of taxicabs to arrive at the house, Chiasson got into his car to drive home. The only thing his teammates at the party saw were headlights pulling away from the house. They were immediately panicked. Minutes later they heard the sirens. Chiasson was killed in a one-car accident that immediately took his life. At the time, he and his wife, Sue, had three young children who, from that night on, grew up without their father. Chiasson's death rocked the NHL community and still serves as a sobering reminder of the cunning aspects of alcoholism and the damage it can leave in its wake.

Another player who impacted me, but in a very subtle way, was defenseman Brad McCrimmon. McCrimmon was nicknamed Beast, a moniker he earned for the direct and often gruff way he spoke to teammates. Brad played in Detroit for just three seasons – 1990-93. During that time I knew him as an intense player but also as a kind and thoughtful man. I always enjoyed going to Brad after a particularly tough game to hear his assessment. His answers to my questions were always straight and to the point ... with thought and without filters. On practice days I enjoyed talking with him, just to experience the warmth of his personality. He would ask about my job, what players I found challenging to talk to, what my deadlines were – selfless questions like that. He took an interest in life outside of himself, and in the world of professional sports that was certainly refreshing.

I remember losing my breath when I learned of Brad's death. After his playing career ended, Brad became a valued assistant coach in the NHL, but the prestigious position of head coach in the league eluded him. So in 2011, he took a job as head coach of Russia's Lokomotiv Yaroslavl team in hopes that it could put his head coaching career on the NHL fast track. But that dream was never realized. The plane carrying the Lokomotiv Yaroslavl team to its first game of the season crashed, killing most onboard, including Brad. It was a stunning and abrupt end of a life with such promise – some realized, but much still to do. I remember feeling that Brad's life was taken far too soon, as if it ended before he could achieve his most notable successes. As with Steve Chiasson, Brad left behind a wife and children who never had the chance to truly know how great a man their father was.

In writing this book, however, I made a discovery that gave me goosebumps and optimism about Brad's life, but more importantly, his death. His lifetime NHL plus/minus rating (the amount of goals scored for his team vs. against his team while he was on the ice) was an astronomical +444. In the NHL, this was considered to be an unfathomable number to reach. In numerology, the numbers 444 signify an angelic presence. Make of that what you will.

Shawn Burr was one of the wittiest people I have ever known and one of the players I thought would live to a ripe old age, telling stories to his grandchildren and great-grandchildren deep into the night. Shawn was a forward who played the majority of his career with the Red Wings. He was drafted in 1984 and was with the Detroit organization until the end of the 1994-95 season. His playing career ended in 2000 with the Tampa Bay organization. But there are no stats that can adequately describe Shawn. Instead, metaphors work best. He was a living, breathing energizer bunny. He talked in the dressing room, on buses, on the ice, on planes. He talked anywhere and anytime someone was there to listen. But what was truly amazing was that much of what he said was either interesting or hilarious. There were fun facts ("My mom says that bananas with brown spots on them have more vitamins in them and you should eat them first."), questions to a teammate ("Hey, which groin did you pull?), and jokes that originally sounded like polite comments ("You can go ahead of me, Cynthia; like my mom always says, 'Dirt before the broom.'").

Being around Shawn was like plopping yourself into the front row of a one-man talk show. He didn't even need a guest because the monologue just kept coming. I often wondered how his brain worked and what would have happened if he, instead of playing professional hockey, had ended up with a desk job … with no one around him to talk with or at. How could he have ever been able to get rid of all of the thoughts coursing through his brain?

It was a joy to watch Shawn in action on the ice, needling opponents with God knows what soliloquies, jokes or putdowns. You could almost see their tempers rise and then finally snap as they lashed out at Shawn, often drawing the only penalty and providing Detroit with a power play.

Years after his retirement from hockey, in 2011, Shawn was diagnosed with myeloid leukemia, which he fought with chemotherapy and a painful bone marrow transplant. Then, in 2013 he suffered a severe brain injury after stumbling down stairs at his home in St. Clair, Michigan. Like Steve Chiasson and Brad McCrimmon, his was an abrupt ending to a larger than life time on this planet. Shawn always seemed like a playful kid to me. His illness and then his passing were both jarring and almost impossible to believe.

Then there was Bob Probert. For those who knew of "Probie" but didn't have the pleasure to talk with him or a front-row seat to see him navigate through his troubled life, he probably seemed like a spoiled athlete who fed on fame and fortune – and that he deserved little sympathy or compassion. But for me, having been around Bob since he was drafted by the Wings in the third round in 1983, his adult life almost seemed like an amusement park ride – one where you sit in the car and think that when you turn the wheel it actually steers your path, but it is just a prop. Instead there is something outside of it guiding it down a predetermined path with a set course, obstacles and duration.

Bob was like a golden retriever puppy – full of mischief, the body too big and gangly for its soul, a good heart that just wants to love and enjoy life, but also a sensitive nature that could be crushed by the wrong influence. On the ice, Bob was a gifted hockey player with the added feature of being one of the most skilled fighters in the history of the game. Despite his playful and sensitive nature, I actually think Bob garnered much of his self-worth from his on-ice brawls. Unlike some other fighters in the NHL, Bob rarely seemed to involve his emotions in the job. Of course, he was passionate about winning every fight, but after the game he was carefree Bob – any animosity left on the ice and just looking to move on with his day or night.

Unfortunately, many of his days and nights became filled with feeding and then battling his well-documented addiction to drugs and alcohol. In his book titled Tough Guy, *Probert's wife, Dani, detailed how reliant her husband was on her to dole out the daily doses of pain medication he needed to manage his various long-term ailments created from years of playing hockey. If she had to go out of town, she would have to hide the doses around the house and then call him to let him know where they were when it was time for him to take them. This was all done because Bob could never trust himself. If left to his own devices, he might binge on the pills and activate his dormant addiction.*

All through Bob's arrest for transporting drugs over the Canadian border into Detroit, his probations, his rehab stays, his relapses and his pain, he was constantly a pleasant person to work with. During my time covering the Wings I had way too many conversations with him about his troubles, his falls, his failures. There never seemed to be the time, the opportunity or the space in the newspaper to talk about the gentleness of Probert – his innocence and kindness, and how I wished to God everyone would just leave the guy alone so he could sort through his illness and truly heal.

I'd like to think Bob found his peace and joy after he retired from the game in 2002. He spent time with his family, rode a motorcycle and cruised on Lake St. Clair on his boat. Bob died in July 2010 after suffering cardiac arrest while boating with his four children and his in-laws. Despite flirting with death for much of his adult life, it was surreal to hear the news of how he died – on a beautiful summer day enjoying one of his passions with many of those closest to him.

Bob crammed a lot of living, suffering, success, failure and love into his 45 years on this earth. And I will always remember him as one of the gentlest and kindest big guys I've ever known.

17

The Final Push

As my seasons on the beat added up I was torn. Though the Red Wings were inching closer and closer to becoming a premier team in the league, my energy levels and enthusiasm for the job began to wane. I started seeing these signs during the 1995-96 season. They showed themselves as mini panic attacks as I packed my suitcase once again to embark on a long road trip, or in the isolation I felt as I spent another night in a hotel room hundreds or thousands of miles from my home. But at the same time, I was eager to see where the Wings' trajectory would deliver them. And I certainly wanted to be there if they ever won the Stanley Cup! So I made a decision to ride it out a little longer. This proved to be one of the greatest decisions of my career.

Fortunately, during this time nothing had changed for the worse with my editors. My job duties were increasing as the Wings climbed in the standings, but so were our readership numbers. On a personal level I could sense this shift by the amount of people who stopped me on the street, at restaurants or at Joe Louis Arena asking for my autograph or a chat about the team. There was a definite momentum building along with a sense of destiny for the team. With the added focus on the Red Wings my nights in the press box were seldom singular affairs anymore. Columnists and sidebar (feature) writers filled the seats next to me. I finally had real colleagues with whom to share the workload.

And by the 1996 playoffs, the staff assembled by *The Detroit News* to cover hockey was an All-Star lineup. To this day I consider it a type of dream team sent out to cover the Wings at home and on the road. Some of the regulars included columnist Bob "Wojo" Wojnowski, feature writer and backup beat writer John "T.W." Niyo, along with outstanding photographers Dan Mears, Jack Gruber and Alan Lessig. Not only were all of these journalists exceptional at their jobs, but they were kind and outrageously fun people to be around.

The six of us jelled right from the start. The photographers were relaxed and saw the world from a different angle than us scribes (and that's not a play on words) ... and they were incredibly funny! That influx of energy was a welcome change and a definite shot of "new" for me. John, the ongoing sidebar writer, and I clicked right from the start. Like the photographers, John was very funny and also had a calming influence over me – something I often needed as I tended to wig-out when faced with unrealistic deadlines or if a player left the locker room before I had the chance to interview him. John's nickname was T.W. because he was pro golfer Tiger Woods' doppelganger. More than once, while covering PGA events, I witnessed John stopped for autographs by excitedly flustered fans who thought he was the golfer.

Wojo had the perfect combination of exceptional writing skills, vast knowledge of all sports and a manner that allowed him to easily connect with the players and coaches. He also had hints of perfectionism and inferiority complex, the latter seeming to drive him to exceptional levels of reporting and writing. This combination made Wojo a valuable member of the NHL coverage team, but also a frequent target of pranks and jokes by the rest of the reporting team. Thankfully, he took each hit with good humor and a vow to get back at the culprits. However, he could never match our creativity, persistence or joy in a successful prank.

Often, Wojo would not travel with the rest of us to road games because he had to hang back to host what we referred to as his "little radio show" on WDFN (The Fan). His broadcast time ran from late afternoon until early evening. As a result, it gave me, John, Dan, Jack and Alan plenty of time to construct our elaborate schemes against him.

One of my favorite pranks was baked during the first round of the playoffs of the 1995-96 season. The Wings faced off against the Winnipeg Jets at Joe Louis Arena for the first two games, then headed to Winnipeg for the next two. For those who have never been to Winnipeg, it's a lovely place – if you like bitter cold temperatures and so much snow that the roads become so narrow they are like tunnels. But Winnipeg is also home to some of the nicest people on the planet. Go figure. This frigid city is located in the southern part of the province of Manitoba, which is situated above North Dakota. I once read that if you travel by car from Winnipeg, heading north for about five hours, you would likely run into polar bears. I'm surprised I didn't see any in Winnipeg during the dead of winter, considering the temperatures were usually hovering around 10- or 20-degrees below zero (Fahrenheit) ... and often dipping below that. This is why it earned the moniker Winter-peg.

On the flight from Detroit to Winnipeg, T.W. and I settled into our seats and listened to the pilot give the weather forecast for Winnipeg. By this time it was April, still the early part of spring, so we weren't expecting balmy. Still, we were hoping for weather that wasn't bone-chilling. But, unfortunately, the high temps in Winnipeg were expected to be in the 20s Fahrenheit. It was the perfect launching pad for the scheme that T.W. and I would plan. Wojo wasn't leaving Detroit for another hour or so. Plenty of time to reach him before he finished packing.

I swiped my credit card to use the airplane phone (yes, primitive days) and we placed an air-to-ground call to Wojo.

"Have you left for the airport yet?" I asked, reaching Wojo on his cell phone.

"Noooo, I'm still packing," he whined. Wojo did this a lot.

"Well, pack light," I said, stifling a giggle as I looked at T.W., who was grinning broadly. "It's supposed to be in the 60s."

Wojo thanked me sincerely. I hung up the phone and noted the $22 charge for that quick phone call. Well worth the price.

Why Wojo would believe us was beyond me and his own fault. When he arrived at the hotel later that night, the full-scale Wojo-whining commenced. For the five days we were in windy and bitter cold Winnipeg, he had one sweater and a light windbreaker type of jacket to go over his button down cotton shirts. Logic would dictate that he would go to a local store and buy a winter coat. Unfortunately, the playoff practice and game schedule was fairly busy, not to mention the copy demands of the job. Wojo had no time to shore up his wardrobe so his only strategy to stay relatively warm was to hurry from the car to the arena, hotel, restaurants and anywhere else we ventured. Oh, and he complained a lot … and vowed that we would rue the day we pulled this prank. We never rued that day. In fact, it only fueled our resolve to create even more elaborate pranks in the future.

That same playoff season marked the identification of our six-person team as a bonded group. After the Wings dispatched the Jets, the next round brought on the St. Louis Blues. Also of note, the spring of 1996 introduced the arrival of the movie *Twister*, a personal favorite of mine considering my love of all things weather related. On an off night in St. Louis, our reporting team went to see the movie. The next day, sitting in the hotel restaurant for breakfast and engaging in our typical jocular behavior, the waitress stopped at our table, smiling.

"You guys remind me of those people in that movie," she said. "You know, *Twister*."

That was the only sign I needed to confirm that our team was, indeed, a special one. To this day, now nearly 20 years after we covered the Stanley Cup in 1998, I have yet to find that kind of connection with coworkers. I guess, in a way, I wouldn't have wanted to try to replicate it. It would take away from the specialness of those friends and what they meant to me, which was a connection I had been missing for years as I covered the Wings as a team of one.

After beating the St. Louis Blues in Game 7 of the Conference semifinal, the Wings moved on to the Conference finals against the Colorado Avalanche. And while many in the league, including me, thought the Wings had a real chance to win it all that year, they fell short, losing to the Avalanche in six games in the best-of-seven series. While I tried to stay objective throughout my career covering the Wings, I have to admit that I felt bad for the players who had such high hopes for a storybook ending to their season. They had finished first in the league – by a wide margin – with an amazing 62-13-7 record for 131 points in 82 games.

Instead of going to the Stanley Cup Finals, they dispersed for a summer of regrets and second-guesses. That, however, only made them stronger the next season. And while their 1996-97 regular season record was a mere shadow of the previous season's, at 38-26-18, what they did was allow for more emotions in the tank for the playoff run. They experienced imperfections and loss during the regular season, all of which proved to shore up their resolve and fill gaps in their game for the postseason, which proved to be a marathon.

The Sisterhood of the Traveling Reporters

Cynthia Lambert

For nearly the first decade of my time as the hockey beat writer for The Detroit News *I was usually the only woman reporter in the press box. The exceptions were if the L.A. Kings, Anaheim Ducks, Boston Bruins, Tampa Bay Lightning or New Jersey Devils came to town. Each of those teams also had a woman covering them – Helene Elliott, Karen Crouse, Nancy Marrapese, Cammy Clark and Sherry Ross, respectively. All of these women were not only pioneers in their own cities and in the NHL, but they all became friends of mine.*

Another welcome exception in the Joe Louis Arena press box and locker room was WDFN sports radio reporter Jennifer Hammond, who came to the Detroit market in 1994. Jennifer is about as solid a reporter as you're going to get, plus she fit in nicely with our Detroit News *dream team of reporters and photographers, often joining us for fun on the road during the 1997 and 1998 Stanley Cup playoffs. By that time she had also caught a freelance gig with local TV station, Fox 2 Detroit, which proved to be the launching pad for her ongoing career at Fox 2.*

In 1995 the rival paper in town, the Detroit Free Press, *hired a woman to take over the hockey beat. Viv Bernstein arrived from Hartford where we had met the year before. Like with the other women reporters, Viv and I became fast friends. So when I got wind that she was taking over the job at the* Freep *I was both happy and cautious. For years it was easy for me to try to scoop the* Freep, *not caring one way or the other for the beat writers there. But now I would be competing against someone I considered a friend. How was this going to work? Though we were friends, we were polar opposites in many ways. I'm tall; Viv is on the shorter side. Viv has short dark hair; I have longer blond hair. She smoked; I didn't. She's Jewish; I'm Catholic.*

Despite our differences, our friendship grew immediately. It began when Viv said she needed to find a place to live in the Detroit area. I invited her to come to my house and I would drive her around the Grosse Pointe area in search of a rental. She was open to living on the east side of Detroit with its close proximity to downtown. As Viv walked into my house I had just finished baking cookies and was in the process of pulling them out of the oven.

"Holy s#@%. You're like Donna friggin' Reed!" she exclaimed, then asked where she could light up. We had a good laugh, got into the car and found her a place to live.

It was also nice to have someone to hang out with on the road. I had never really felt comfortable infusing myself into lunches or dinners with the male reporters or broadcasters in the years before. And I'm not one of those people who likes going to a restaurant by herself; just too self-conscious I suppose. As a result, I ate a lot of room service meals and saw every movie available on hotel TV.

During longer road trips, Viv and I would meet for dinner or go to a local event. Our most memorable excursion came while the Wings were in Calgary for a few days. It was odd but nice to have more than one day off on the road, so after the practice ended and we wrote our articles for the next day, Viv and I decided to drive to picturesque Banff for dinner. I rented a car and we headed out to the ski resort area, which was less than a two hour drive away. The trip there was breathtaking as we wound our way up the mountainous road. Dinner was also nice, but during the meal a light snow began to fall. By the time we were done and on the road back, a few inches had accumulated. Then, as we made our way along Highway 1 – the only road back to Calgary – traffic began to slow as conditions worsened. It was turning in to a blizzard with whiteout conditions. Beneath the tires, the highway was also icing over. Since we were in the mountains the last thing anyone wanted to do was spin out of control and over the edge. No one could see the lane lines so driving was treacherous.

After about an hour I started getting the urge to pee. Surely the weather would clear up soon, I reasoned. Another half hour passed and we moved only a few yards. Then came the flashing lights of the police. Traffic was at a standstill by this time and motorists were getting out of their cars to investigate the delay. Slowly, word trickled to us – a truck had jackknifed and the road was closed. No estimate of when it would reopen. By this time I had to pee REALLY badly. Viv kept talking about how cool the snow was.

"Look at how fast it's coming at the windshield!" she marveled, trying to distract me from my bursting bladder but still laughing at me.

I couldn't even look at the snow. All my focus had to go into controlling my bladder. About another hour later, the whiteout subsided and traffic started to move. When I finally pulled up in front of the hotel it was all I could do to grunt out my question to the man at the front desk.

"Where is the restroom?" I begged.

My relief of seeing the inside of that bathroom stall was one I will never forget … that and my pride in the strength of my bladder.

18

Winning ... and Loss

The road to the Cup in the 1996-97 postseason went through Anaheim and St. Louis before landing the Wings once again in Colorado for the Conference finals. But this time, it was the Wings who came out on top in six games over the Avs. It then set them up for the most exhilarating high followed by the most horrific low.

The Red Wings matched up against the big Philadelphia Flyers, who had home-ice advantage for the Stanley Cup Finals. That meant the Wings were on the road for the first two games, then back at Joe Louis Arena for the next two to kick off the series. Remarkably, the Wings defeated the Flyers by 4-2 scores in the first two games, then routed them 6-1 in the first game back at Joe Louis Arena. Suddenly, within a week, the Wings were one win away from achieving the NHL pinnacle – the Stanley Cup. A few hours before the matinee Game 4 was to begin I parked my car in *The Detroit News* lot, which was about a half mile walk to the arena. I figured if the Wings won I didn't want to get caught in the jubilation and traffic in the streets surrounding Joe Louis. It was an exceptional decision, as Detroit won 2-1 to sweep the Flyers for the Stanley Cup win, the first for Detroit in 42 years.

One of my fondest memories of that game and playoff run came afterwards in the Red Wings dressing room. Of course, all of the players were celebrating, drinking champagne from the Cup and hoisting it over their heads for photo opportunities. It was a scene of nonstop jubilation after a 10-month marathon. The player most out of character was the usually stoic and quiet Russian-born defenseman Vladimir Konstantinov. Vlady wasn't grumpy or mean; his demeanor was more reserved and thoughtful. But not on this night. Instead, Vlady ran around the locker room shouting louder than I had ever heard him: "He shoots, he scores! He shoots he scores!!" His unbridled enthusiasm was noticed by anyone within earshot. Most, like me, couldn't help but smile as they observed this exceptional hockey talent officially breaking out of his measured and reserved shell. As he made the rounds with his jubilation, he came up to me, grabbed my shoulders with his champagne- and sweat-soaked hands and yelled into my face, "Cyndy! He shoots, he scores!" Then he shook me loose and headed on to his next victim. He was happiness personified.

Six days after that celebratory moment came the night that changed everything, and shortened the well-deserved revelry earned by those in the Red Wings organization. Konstsantinov, along with teammate and hockey icon Viacheslav Fetisov and team masseur Sergei Mnatsakanov, rode in the back of a limousine on the way home from a Stanley Cup celebration. The summer was going to be filled with Cup celebrations; this was one of the first. These pop-up parties were happening all over the city as the trophy made its way through the Red Wings lineup, allowing each player or member of the organization some alone time with the prize.

Fetisov, Konstantinov and Mnatsakanov knew they would want to drink and celebrate, so they rented a limo. They weren't about to take any chances getting behind the wheel of a car after a night of drinking. Unfortunately, the man who did get behind the wheel of the limousine, Richard Gnida, was in no shape to drive. Gnida was operating the limo – unbeknownst to the men riding in the back – with a suspended license. It was suspended because of a drunk driving violation. On this fateful night, Gnida fell asleep at the wheel. As the limousine sped down the road it careened off its path at a high speed, smashing headfirst into a tree. Fetisov, Konstantinov and Mnatsakanov were thrown at an equally high velocity like ragdolls from their seats to the front end of the limo cabin. It's hard to even comprehend what it was like for the three men, feeling the thrill of hockey's greatest accomplishment one moment and unbearable pain and devastation the next.

I knew nothing about the accident until my phone rang. I had planned on getting to bed early, as I was still trying to catch up on my sleep from the long playoff haul. I almost didn't answer the phone, not wanting to be tempted to go out or stay up later talking. But something told me to pick up. I did. I was greeted by the voice of Toronto-based reporter Al Strachan.

"Have you heard?" Al asked me.

"Heard what?" I replied, thinking perhaps the Wings had made a trade.

"It's all over the (press) wire," Al continued. "There's been an accident – Fetisov, Konstantinov and the team masseur. No one knows how bad it is, or if anyone was killed."

I thanked Al for calling, hung up and called the office. They, too, were hearing the initial reports about the accident.

"Stay by your phone," I was ordered by my editor.

Moments later Wojo called. I told him all I knew and he shared his information with me. We had both heard that the three men were taken to Beaumont Hospital in the suburb of Royal Oak. We agreed to meet there.

By the time I arrived at the hospital, fans were gathering outside. Security personnel were closely guarding access into the hospital. We showed our Red Wings press badges and were admitted. There we waited with dozens of other reporters, photographers and film crews, all the while trying to piece together the events of the night that led to our gathering at the hospital. When they had information to report, hospital spokespeople addressed the media gathered. The news was not good for any of the victims.

Reporters are supposed to be impartial, but that isn't a synonym for uncaring. As we stood, waiting for more news, I remember praying that this would all resolve itself positively. That the best case scenarios for all three men would fall into place. I couldn't bear to think of them dealing with long-term injuries for the rest of their lives. But, unfortunately, this happened for two of the three.

Fetisov sustained a bruised lung and chest contusions. Mnatsakanov was paralyzed from the waist down and also sustained head injuries. Konstantinov's injuries were primarily to his brain, and he was placed on a ventilator. The Vlady who shouted at the top of his lungs in celebration less than a week before was now trapped inside a man's body that was not – could not – remember how to speak or walk, let alone breathe. But the warrior in Vlady has powered his progress over the years. Though his recovery has been steady, albeit incremental, the left frontal lobe of his brain was forever destroyed in the accident.

The limo accident, and having to cover it from a news perspective, broke my heart. True, I was not part of the Red Wings team, but I saw those players more than my own family. I was there for many of their highest highs and lowest lows, asking them to talk about how they felt, to share with me the depths of their emotions and to trust me with their words. You don't do that kind of job and leave your feelings about them as people – not just hockey players – out of the picture. My heart went out to the players and their families, especially those belonging to Konstantinov and Mnatsakanov. I did the best I could to cover the accident that night, staying at the hospital well into the morning hours to hear firsthand what the doctors and other specialists had to say.

Days later, I returned to Joe Louis Arena to "cover" the Red Wings players emptying out their lockers. A car was parked in the lower concourse, outside the hallway leading to the locker room. As I approached, the car door opened and Fetisov stepped out. He moved slowly, his face still marked with the effects of the accident and his steps deliberate so as not to disturb his body's physical healing.

As I approached him, having no idea what I could say about his wellbeing and that of his friends', he opened his arms and hugged me. There was no objective reporting to be done at that moment. To not allow sentiment to take over would have been inhumane. As we separated, he shook his head. I told him how terribly sorry I was for all he and the others had been through. I think I jotted down some of the comments he made, but to pursue more, I believed, would have been disrespectful.

In the years since that time, I have had the pleasure of seeing Mnatsakanov and his wife at the local pool, discovering after the accident that we lived just about a mile from each other. The year after the accident I saw Konstantinov a few times when he was brought to the arena. It was heartbreaking to see him struggle to control his body and to see his distant look. On a positive note, in the years since then "Vlady" has made significant gains in his health, again, a testament to his drive and strength.

Feeling Welcomed

Cynthia Lambert

I am grateful to say that my life inside the Red Wings locker room was a positive and productive work environment. In a very weird way it was a home away from home; I knew where everything was, understood who was always willing to talk no matter what, and how to approach a player for an explanation and a quote after he screwed up during a game. In a sense it was my home turf, sometimes even more than The Detroit News *sports department because of the sheer number of hours I spent in there.*

Despite the length of my reporting career, I know I would not have lasted beyond a few seasons if it wasn't for the overwhelming acceptance by the players and coaches. If there were players who didn't respect or like me, they kept those feelings well hidden under the veil of professionalism. Led by the examples of Yzerman and superstar defenseman Nicklas Lidstrom, other members of the team emulated this professionalism. A few rise to the surface in my mind as being particularly welcoming.

Dino Ciccarelli

Dino Ciccarelli arrived in Detroit from the Washington Capitals with baggage. He had already served jail time for hitting a player in the head with his stick, and there were also allegations of criminal sexual conduct. Whether he was guilty or not, I was not going to respect or like him. I would cover his play as part of the Red Wings, but that was it.

Then I met him. I tried my hardest to be cold to him but there was something about his surly and self-deprecating nature that was implicitly raw and honest. He gave off the energy of someone who had been kicked and knocked down repeatedly, but somehow had the ability to get back up. After a year or so, Dino was a favorite of mine. One time in particular, before a road game, Dino was in the hall outside the locker room by himself, fixing the blow torch to the blade of one of his sticks to get the perfect arc. An old radio sat on the table contributing background music as Dino worked. Then he started singing. The song was "Loser" by Beck.

"I'm a loser baby, so why don't you kill me," Dino sang out, looking at me. Then he spoke. "I'm too old for this, Cyndy. I'm a loser."

Dino was 32 years old at the time.

Chris Osgood

Chris always seemed like a kid to me, one who needed to be dealt with kindly. He didn't arrive in the NHL with talent oozing from his pores. Instead, he took the sizeable talent that he did have and worked extremely hard to climb to the top of his field. That is admirable in any line of work, but especially under the spotlight of a professional sport.

One of my favorite Chris moments came one spring when I told him about the kids living on my block in Grosse Pointe Woods. Every day after school and on the weekends they filled a section of the street to play hockey — some wearing inline skates, others running in athletic shoes as they chased the ball or street hockey disc. They all wore Red Wings t-shirts or jerseys and many of them donned the No. 30 that belonged to Chris. He listened to me tell the story then surprised me by asking for the address and directions.

"Can you imagine how excited they would be if I just stopped by and played some hockey with them?" he asked. "If an NHL player came by my neighborhood growing up it would have blown me away."

For a couple of weeks Chris tried to coordinate when he could stop by, but we could never sync up our schedules. After that, the playoffs started, eliminating all extraneous time. Just the fact that Chris understood the impact he could have on kids who adored him told me that he hadn't forgotten who he was and where he came from.

Kirk Maltby

When I decided to leave my job at The News, *I lost a good part of my identity. "Cynthia Lambert" and "Red Wings beat writer" were two terms that went hand in hand in my mind. Who was I if I wasn't a reporter? One day, shortly after stepping away from my career, I went into the Caribou Coffee shop in my neighborhood and did a double take. Wings forward Kirk Maltby stood in front of me in line. When he saw me he broke into a smile and started a conversation. It was the first time I had spoken with a player since leaving my job and my "role." It was a whole different world asking questions and not measuring the answers against their newsworthiness.*

Over the past 20 years I have seen Kirk, now a scout for the Wings, at neighborhood coffee shops and even on Halloween, as his children often went trick or treating on my block. It's been nice having that loose connection to my "past life."

Kevin Allen

My life as a sports reporter included friendships and acquaintances with dozens of reporters, photographers and TV sports personalities. And while I am grateful to so many of them for their support and camaraderie, one stands out to me: USA Today's *Kevin Allen.*

Kevin was on the NHL beat before I began my career in the mid-1980s and, as of this writing in 2017, he's still on it. Despite his rigorous schedule and the decades of deadlines that have come and gone, he has remained a hockey sage with a curiosity about the sport and its personalities that hasn't waned. I was fortunate to see him and benefit from his positive outlook often throughout my career; he lives in the Detroit area, meaning he used Joe Louis Arena as his home base of sorts.

Kevin showed me – by example – how to feed my curiosity about the sport and conduct a professional interview. He also showed me what respect from professional athletes looks like. On more than one occasion he would offer me feedback on how he observed players reacting to me – usually highlighting the positive. The icing on the cake was his undying support of me as a reporter, and for that, I will always be grateful.

19

Breakaway

At the start of the next season, the 1997-98 campaign, I met Jerry Nehr, the man I would eventually marry. That growing relationship, combined with my growing fatigue of the rigors of being a beat reporter caused me to start seeing glimpses of the finish line of my career. And it seemed as though my body was breaking down, giving me another sign that the end of this job was near. In January of 1998 I herniated a disc in my neck. It was likely the result of carrying too much on my shoulders – not problems, but luggage, computers, reference books, etc. for more than a decade.

Because I needed to go to physical therapy three times a week – and had received a strong admonition from my doctor not to travel – I stayed home. It was the first time in 12 years that I didn't have a stack of airplane tickets sitting on my kitchen counter. And I loved the feeling. I took my suitcase from its constant position in the corner of my bedroom and moved it in to the attic storage. I went to the grocery store and bought food for two weeks instead of just for a couple of days. I accepted invitations to dinners and parties. It was a normal existence.

To this day I feel that the herniated disc and subsequent physical therapy time commitment were cosmic messages. They were meant to guide me in a new direction, one that would open up more joy and fulfillment rather than adding on more years performing the same job. In addition to the ability to stay home, I also got a flavor of what it was like to live without the stress of a daily deadline, as *The News* had assigned an interim reporter to cover the road trips. I had no idea how much I had missed a "normal" life.

Physical therapy over and neck healed, I rejoined the beat in mid-March of 1998 ... just in time for the playoffs. While the Red Wings were favored by many to repeat as Cup champions, the big question mark was whether they could do it without Konstantinov, and whether the weight of what transpired the summer before would vault the Wings to victory once again or pull them down. The team, guided by Coach Scotty Bowman, did the former, winning the first three rounds against Phoenix, St. Louis and Dallas in six games each. The Wings then swept the Washington Capitals in the Cup finals to win back-to-back Stanley Cups, a rare feat. This time the clinching win came on the road and the celebration was something that was inspiring yet sad. Instead of taking the victory lap with the Cup in his arms, Yzerman presented it to Konstantinov who was transported out onto the ice in a wheelchair. The team then followed Konstantinov, pushed from behind by Fetisov, around the ice in celebration.

Having covered back-to-back Stanley Cups, enjoying a blossoming relationship with my future husband and feeling a growing sense of unease about my job, I knew I had to make a decision. The whole summer after the 1998 Cup win for me was spent agonizing over whether to step down off the beat and stay on as a general sports reporter, or to leave *The Detroit News* completely and start a new career.

I had very little confusion about whether I needed to step down from the beat. To me, this was the perfect time to walk away. I reported on the Wings from the time when they were the worst team in the league to now, the best. I wrestled with my next step for months, unsure whether I should give up this career of a lifetime, knowing full well I would never get it back – at least not in Detroit. Then there was the question of what I would do for a living. I interviewed at community newspapers, but the pay was not sufficient for me to maintain the lifestyle to which I had grown accustomed. What else was I qualified to do? Writing and reporting was all I knew.

I felt strongly that I wanted to do something I felt passionate about. Since my mother's death, I was interested in working to help in cancer prevention. So I placed a call to Peter Karmanos, Jr. Pete had recently donated $15 million to the Michigan Cancer Foundation in downtown Detroit in honor of his first wife, who passed away from breast cancer (the health facility was then renamed the Barbara Ann Karmanos Cancer Institute). Pete was also owner of the Carolina Hurricanes NHL franchise, formerly the Hartford Whalers. Because of this connection, I had intermittently interviewed Pete about hockey business for years and admired the way he worked. I found his unbridled honesty and passion for the game to be refreshing.

I phoned Pete at his executive office at Compuware Corporation – the software and services company he co-founded in the early 1970s – sharing with him my situation and thoughts. I asked if there might be a job opening at the Barbara Ann Karmanos Cancer Institute.

"I don't know about there, but why don't you come work for me here?" was his reply.

This took me by surprise, to be sure. Compuware was a technology and professional services company for mainframe and distributed computer systems. I could hardly grasp what "mainframe" or "distributed" meant, let alone write about it to employees. I might as well be hired by NASA to explain methods of determining whether there is water on Mars, or what the rock formations on the moon mean. But I needed a job.

I agreed to interview with someone from Compuware's communications department and simultaneously applied at the Karmanos Cancer Institute. A week later I had a job offer from Compuware and I took it.

The conversation with my boss, Phil Laciura, at *The News*

did not go as well as I had hoped. Phil had been one of my most ardent supporters at the paper right from the beginning, guiding me throughout my career, pushing me to be a better and tougher reporter. He never questioned my abilities. He was the one who threw me my early writing assignments and defended me to the non-believers on the staff. But I couldn't string this out any longer. I knew I had lost the spark of competitiveness needed to do the job of a beat reporter well. Phil and I both knew this. But when I told him I had found another job, he seemed stunned.

"Why are you leaving this, Lambert?" he asked.

I told him my reasons, which he didn't fully buy, I'm sure. More time at home. Tired. Want a family. Want to get away from the stress and pressure.

He finally accepted my resignation, but added a comment of warning: "I think you're going to regret this decision," he said.

I cried all the way home. What did I just do? How could I walk away from a job that I once said I would do for free? How many people have that in their life? I was quitting at the top of my career. Don't people usually walk away when they can't do a job anymore, not when they're in their prime and just tired?

But after seeing more than 1,200 hockey games and four or five times as many practices in 12 years, I did walk away. And I am happy to report that I never once regretted the decision. I got married the next year and two years later gave birth (just before turning 40 years old) to Quinn, the most amazing son I could ever hope for. I've been to a handful of Wings games in the years since I left. I enjoy them but it feels good to walk out with the masses and head home.

More often I head to Comerica Park to watch the Detroit Tigers. It's a return to the first sport I played and you get to sit outside! There are times when the Wings hold practices at the ice rink at my son's school. Sometimes he wanders over to watch for a bit, and comes home talking about the speed of the players and the game ... and part of me is jealous. I've asked him to text me when the Wings are skating at his school, just in case I want to drive over and see world-class players, and experience the speed of the game, the brutality of the hits and the amazing game that is hockey.

But I haven't yet gone. I'm almost afraid to open that door and start pining for the thrill of the reporting game again. So I stay away and focus on my current job – as a mom and communications specialist at Henry Ford Health System. Now I write to inform doctors and nurses of things they need to know to make their jobs and lives easier. It's a career that makes me feel good about myself. I am helping people who save lives. And I don't have to get on a plane or stay out until midnight to do it well.

POST SCRIPT

For 14 years I had the best job in the world.

Nearly 20 years after I left my position as Red Wings and NHL writer for *The Detroit News*, I still have fond memories of my "beat" days. I believe the gift of time helped me clear away the clutter of frustration and fatigue to create a memoir of sorts that, hopefully, offers a true picture of what it was like for me to be among the first wave of female sports reporters in Detroit.

Time also offered me the opportunity to forget the looks on players' faces as I approached them to talk about subjects they'd rather avoid. It took a lot of courage and fortitude on my part to know that I was often unwanted – not because of who I was but due to the role I served. I had a job to do. It's a challenge faced by every reporter. Some reporters relish those looks of distain on their interviewees, others grudgingly deal with them. I was certainly in the latter category.

I was blessed to cover a team filled to the brim with class. Not every reporter can say that but I most assuredly can. And I also covered a sport with interesting and mostly compliant people from the shores of Vancouver and Los Angeles to the urban settings of New York, Chicago and Toronto and all points in between. Hockey people really are different. There is a thread of courtesy woven into every team, while the sense of entitlement seen so prevalently in the world of professional sports is often missing ... thank God.

Through this process of writing I have come to understand that when I left the hockey beat in November of 1998 it was more of a fleeing than a stepping away. It was kind of like a story my friend Paula Wetzel told me one time about an oyster bake she attended. As she sat on the beach eating oysters, she relished every taste and nuance. She ate more than she thought she would because they tasted so good. As she forked the umpteenth oyster into her mouth she suddenly realized she couldn't swallow it. She had reached an uncomfortable – but definite – limit.

My last oyster was the Stanley Cup finals of 1998. I had seen the Red Wings team go from being the worst in the league in 1986 to winning back-to-back Stanley Cups – a mini-dynasty. My career had also progressed to the point where I was satisfied that there was little more I could do to eclipse what I had already accomplished. I was known throughout North America, wrote for *The Hockey News*, contributed to *Sports Illustrated*, and was on local and national TV and radio. I was ready to move on to my next challenge.

I will be forever grateful to *The Detroit News* for taking a chance on me, to see what I could accomplish and for sticking with me in the early, learning years. I am also thankful to all who helped me along the way, including *News* colleagues Bob Wojnowski, John Niyo, Dan Mears, Jack Gruber and Alan Lessig, and to my fellow hockey reporter friends around North America for offering me friendship and support along the way.

I would be remiss if I did not mention the fans of Detroit Red Wings hockey for accepting me and my words. Had you resisted getting your hockey news from a woman my career would have been stopped short, to be sure. As legendary Detroit musician Bob Seger pointed out in his *Live Bullet* album, *Rolling Stone* magazine said that Detroit audiences are the greatest rock and roll audiences in the world. But I say Detroit has the greatest sports fans in the world. From the bottom of my heart, thank you for letting me be a part of it.

With gratitude and thanks,
Cynthia Lambert

ABOUT THE AUTHOR

Cynthia Lambert entered the field of sports reporting at a time when it was still new and novel for women to have access to the interior of a locker room. Fresh out of college and driven by an internal force, she overcame biases and hurdles to become one of the Detroit area's first female "beat" writers, covering the Detroit Red Wings for 12 seasons, from 1986-98.